Closer to Paradise

• • • •

A Mother's Journey through Crisis and Healing

To Suzanne With Big Love Amy

Amy White

MOtivational PRESS®
LEADERS IN GLOBAL PUBLISHING

Published by Motivational Press, Inc.
1777 Aurora Road
Melbourne, Florida, 32935
www.MotivationalPress.com

Manufactured in the United States of America.

ISBN: 978-1-62865-309-0

Contents

• • • •

To my boys, may they always know in their hearts how much they are loved.

Foreword

• • • •

Pain can be unspeakable at times. To find the words to describe its depth, intensity, and grip is often unfathomable. As a mother, woman, and teacher, I am deeply moved and inspired by Amy White's commitment to give voice to her pain, to mental illness, and to the stigma associated with mental health.

I first met Amy when I interviewed her for Women For One's "Real Women, Courageous Wisdom" podcast series. She is an intuitive coach, a Caregiver champion, and international bestselling author of *Bold is Beautiful: Breakthrough to Business Strategies.* In her first book, Amy shared her story of leaving her career to pursue the dream of coaching and advocating for parents, caregivers, and those transitioning through life's challenges and crises. Now, in *Closer to Paradise: A Mother's Journey through Crisis and Healing,* Amy boldly and courageously shares her experience as a caregiver during her son's mental health crisis.

In sharing her journey, Amy brings you directly to the front lines of her son's illness and her countless battles as she desperately tries to secure care and treatment for her son. Ultimately, however, *Closer to Paradise* is Amy's story of personal revolution. She shares the depth of her own mental pain as she watches her son's health deteriorate and fights to keep him safe. Amy also lets us into the heartbreaking process of what it means to truly let go. She speaks of the intense challenges of parenting and her sense of failure as a mother. Amy's resolve to "seal the cracks" in her own heart leads her to find creative and meaningful ways to break the silence about mental illness and support others in crisis in the process.

In essence, Amy's story of resilience, strength, and determination models what I call "being fully alive," which means showing up fully for all moments of our life, even the most painfully dark and excruciating ones. By showing up in every moment of her son's crisis, Amy has not only found healing for herself but she has filled a tremendous gap in our society by advocating for mental health and offering other parents and caregivers a playbook of pitfalls and lessons learned from her own trials and challenges.

The story Amy tells could not be further from paradise, but the life she has formed on the other side of crisis is powerfully hopeful that paradise is possible after pain.

Cara Bradley, Author, Teacher, Entrepreneur, Wayne, PA
On the Verge: Wake Up, Show Up, and Shine (New World Library, 2016)

Introduction

• • • •

U ntil the moment I stepped into the Psychiatric Emergency Department at our local hospital, I had no idea the speed of my son's breakdown. I was totally and completely floored. It wasn't as though I didn't know he was depressed; he'd been in counseling for years. I knew he disliked school and I had made several attempts to help find him alternatives. I knew he was using drugs and had tried drug counseling, therapy and testing. I created consequences and handed out rewards to motivate him to stay clean and sober. I knew when he was lying to me. I saw the decline, the isolation and the mood changes but, honestly, I thought it was normal teenage stress and that he would move through it as I had when I had played the role of dark, tormented teenager some years before.

As a parent, I was engaged. I listened. I met with his school counselor and his therapist. When he said he wanted to feel useful, I found him volunteer opportunities. When music was the antidote, I bought him a bass guitar and lessons. I did all I could think of to support him and counteract the speed of his decline. I hoped that if I could just get him through high school, he would see that there was a huge world out there full of so much promise and possibility. And yet, in the end, I never saw his breakdown coming.

The road to my son's recovery was long and winding, with many twists and turns. The first steps were to stabilize the situation and later to feel all of the sadness, fear and pain associated with what he - and in turn what I - experienced. I still experience some post-traumatic symptoms as a result. I am still healing from this experience. The good news is that I am healing each and every day. I have come to a place within that trusts that my son needs to do this journey his way - a way that I cannot direct nor influence. I can be there with a big, open heart, an open mind, and the daily belief that we are moving through this together.

What started out solely as an intention to support my son through his mental health crisis has become a journey that opened the doors for self-exploration, forgiveness and healing for me.

My journey towards a more authentic self had started years ago, long before this crisis. It started at the point where I realized my own life had spiraled out of control. I was a single parent, working to support my children's needs and wants, trying to regain "control" of my life after a bitter divorce laden with enough negative muck to last lifetimes. I'd lay in bed at the end of the day, exhausted and depressed, wondering how things had gone so far off the rails. I remember the exact moment when I called out to the Universe, my soul, and any higher power that might be listening, asking what I needed to do to find peace in my life and to bring peace to my children's lives as well. That night, I heard an answer loud and clear: I needed to learn to love myself. Unfortunately, it would take my child's mental health breakdown before I was ready to listen.

As a result of this crisis, I realized and recognized that I carried so much of my own pain with me as well. This pain was not a result of my son's crisis but the recognition of it, the calling it by name, was a result of it. It offered me the opportunity to pull back the layers of blame and shame, to look stigma and misconceptions directly in the eyes and learn to love myself in a way that I never thought possible. Forgiveness. Acceptance. Trust. A long, painful road, and one that required me to look at my "stuff" from a whole new level, yet also one that gave me an opportunity to seal the cracks in my own heart so that I could love myself, my children and others with a ferocious love. I just had to be willing to take the journey.

Chapter 1

• • • •

Josh's birthday that year was fun and significant for him. It was his sixteenth. I excused him from school for a few hours that day so that he could get his driver's permit. We laughed and joked all the way to the Department of Motor Vehicles. Josh picked on me for my driving and teased me about being such a "rule follower," especially when I exceeded the speed limit. He was really in his element, full of smiles and talking non-stop. I am sure that it was because he was excited to be out of school but, even so, it filled my heart with great joy to share this time with him.

Since he hadn't studied at all for the permit test, we knew that it would be an interesting experience one way or the other. Josh must have seen the worry on my face. "I've got this Mom," he said. I'm not sure either one of us really believed it, but there was no turning back at that point, and into the testing room he went. As I watched, I felt my heart fill with love and gratitude for this boy turning into a man right before my eyes.

When the test was complete, Josh and I stood together at the desk while the proctor checked his answers. "Wow, I've gotten quite a few wrong, Mom," Josh shared quietly under his breath as we watched the results unfold in front of us. His anticipation was palpable and the air felt almost electric. As luck would have it, he passed and as the paperwork was being processed, we high-fived and hugged right in the middle the lobby; neither of us cared that we were making quite a scene. It made me so happy to see him so excited and positive about his accomplishment and his future. I felt such great pride, proud that he had taken the test and passed it even though he chose to do no preparation. I also felt such relief and gratitude that this experience had been so positive especially since over the past several weeks, Josh's disposition had become dark and depressed.

When we left the DMV, it was snowing, a stark contrast to the sunny cloudless sky we experienced driving there. Josh wasn't comfortable driving, so I drove. Josh never missed an opportunity for a little more time out of school. "You know Mom, since I'm going to miss my lunch hour anyway, wouldn't it be nice to stop and have some lunch together?" he said, smiling smugly. He knew I couldn't pass up an invitation to spend a little more time with him. On the way back to school, we stopped off for lunch and shared more jokes and laughter. That day filled my heart up full.

Those moments of joy and celebration would not last for long. Over the next couple of weeks, Josh's mood continued to spiral downward. When I tried to talk with him about what was going on, his responses were always angry. "Mom, I told you I'm depressed and you don't want to believe me." I did believe him; I was taking his feelings very seriously. I just wasn't sure how to help and, given the angry way Josh was choosing to address it with me, it was obvious that I was not meeting his expectations.

Josh had started to show signs of decline just after the first weeks of school. He had such a great experience over the summer working as a camp counselor and came home full of inspiration and motivation to make that coming school year his best ever. Unfortunately, this excitement quickly turned to disdain, and as the weeks passed his mood continued to worsen.

The downward slide had started to escalate in the weeks before his birthday. It began when Josh announced his desire to begin taking antidepressants. This declaration had taken me by surprise. While his mood had grown darker and more agitated in those weeks, I had not been in favor of him taking medication because I was concerned about the side effects. Still, we sought out the advice of his doctor and agreed to start Josh on a low-dose of Zoloft as a trial. Within days of starting the medication, Josh's agitation turned to anger and then the anger turned to rage. During one incident, he punched the wall so hard that we ended up in the emergency room for x-rays, fearing he'd broken his hand.

Concerned about the side effects, Josh's doctor recommended discontinuation of the Zoloft and provided a referral for a full assessment with an adolescent psychiatric specialist.

With his psychiatrist appointment scheduled for a couple of weeks after his birthday, I remained hopeful that this would be the turning point to get him back on track. In my mind, I kept trying to fit all of the pieces to this difficult puzzle together. I couldn't understand what was happening to Josh and how we could go from having such a joy-filled celebration on his birthday to the place where the angst and dark mood once again was front and center in our lives. With the exception of the brief positive experience on his birthday, it felt like he was sinking into quicksand. I didn't know what else to do to help him. I didn't know how to counteract this slide.

On the afternoon of his first appointment with the psychiatrist, I received a text from Josh. It read, "Don't worry about me. I'll be home later." Panic filled my body. I responded a few times, asking him to let me know what was going on and reminding him that he had an appointment that afternoon, but I received no response. I tried to call his phone, but there was no answer. I continued to text him. "Josh, please tell me what is going on!" and still received no response. As the afternoon grew late and the appointment time approached, I decided to drive to his high school, since that was the last place he had been, and see if I could find out what was going on. Josh often stayed after school so that he could hang out with his girlfriend, so the fact that he was late wasn't as concerning as the fact that he wasn't responding to my attempts to contact him.

Three sheriff's cars passed me, heading in the same direction as the school. At first I thought nothing of it, but as I turned into the parking lot of the school and saw the officers' cars, I knew something was wrong. My heart sank and panic rose in my body. I turned into the front lot where the police were parked and got out of my car. A man I didn't recognize began yelling at me over the wind and sleeting rain. I could tell by his face that he was angry, but I could not hear his words. A sheriff approached me as I stood outside my car, shaking partially from the cold, wet weather but mostly because I couldn't understand what was happening. I feared the worst.

The man in the parking lot turned out to be Josh's girlfriend's guardian. We were at the school for the same reason, and the story began to unfold: the sheriff informed me that Josh and his girlfriend had run away. Since it was the beginning of winter, they had made it several miles away to a local mall and had stopped to figure out their next move. Josh had contacted his older brother, Aaron, for help and, ultimately, his father had gotten involved to bring the kids home.

One of the officers pulled me aside to try to help me understand what had happened. Standing inside the entryway of my son's high school, this stern but kind-looking officer began to explain that Josh was running away because he could no longer take the turmoil and fighting in our home. As Officer Martinez relayed the facts as he knew them, I could feel the blood drain my face. He asked me, "Do you know why they ran away? Has there been on-going trouble in your household?" In disbelief, I shook my head no. The officer seemed visibly surprised by my answers. The look on his face softened as he realized that the stories were not lining up. He said, "Josh had made it very clear to the officer in charge that the fighting between the two of you was unbearable." He went on to explain that Josh felt that he could not rely on me, which, he explained, was why he called his brother for support.

I was shocked. In my mind, there was no constant fighting or turmoil between us. We had a very close relationship and, with the exception of addressing some recreational drug use during the prior year, there had been no real issues between us. I knew that when I had addressed Josh's drug use with a surprise intervention that included his brother, father and stepmother, our relationship had changed. Josh felt betrayed by me, even though I was doing what I thought was best for him. After that experience, though, things were not bad between us. Josh had become a bit more distant with me, but it was only in the weeks prior to his birthday that there had been any real challenges in our relationship.

My mind was exploding. I was completely in shock. I could not understand how this was happening. In my mind, there had been no clear indications that my son felt so much anger towards me.

Out of the corner of my eye, I noticed Josh was there at the school, sitting on the floor in the corner on the other side of the entry hallway. He must have arrived through a different doorway while I was speaking with the officer. Josh's sandy-brown hair was matted to his head and he looked much smaller than his six foot, athletic build. His deep brown eyes looked almost black in the florescent overhead lighting. He looked scared. I wanted to run to him and cradle him in my arms, but his father and brother encircled him. Given this new information, I wasn't sure how to act. Officer Martinez approached Josh, saying that he needed to ask him a few questions. Through my confusion, I tried to listen to the exchange between Josh and the officer. My mind was having a tough time comprehending the whole situation. As I listened to Josh's answers, I began to realize that he was feeling unwell. "I have been feeling very depressed lately. No, I'm not sleeping well. The constant fighting makes things worse," he shared. The turmoil he felt existed at home was only acting to aggravate his feelings of despair. I wasn't prepared for the next revelation. There, on the floor of his high school, Josh said, "I feel like I should be hospitalized because I'm afraid I might hurt myself." I heard my heart thumping in my ears and thought for a moment I might physically fall to my knees.

Scared that he would be admitted to the hospital and would not be home for Christmas - just two days away - he wasn't sure that he wanted to go to the hospital that night. My heart was torn. I understood how important the holiday was for Josh but, as I watched him there on the floor, still cowering in the corner, vacillating between anger and tears, there was no way that I was going to leave him unchecked. I asked him again if he felt that he was safe. He maintained that he truly felt unsafe and unwell. I decided to take him to the emergency department of our local hospital after a stop home for some dry clothes.

Chapter 2

• • • •

While I waited for Josh to collect some of his belongings before we made the drive to the emergency room, Christmas carolers came to our door. I looked into the faces of my neighbors and their children singing their hearts out in joy and exultation on our front steps while my heart was shattering. I could not grasp the concept of 'Joy to the World' in that moment; in fact, it would be a very long time before I would feel joy again.

I had been to the emergency room a few times with my children over the years, mostly for falls, sports injuries and one nasty dog bite, but nothing prepared me for what I was about to experience as we went through check-in with the triage nurse.

After the basic set of pre-admission questions, we waited to be seen by a doctor. Expecting a nurse to come show Josh to an exam room, we were instead met by a security guard who escorted us down a short corridor. The guard took all of Josh's personal effects, including his shoes, and scanned him with a handheld metal detector. Standing in that back hallway, not far from the registration desk, it was unnerving to watch Josh being searched. Surprisingly, Josh took much of it in stride until the guard asked for his iPod. "Music is how I calm my nerves," Josh protested. I offered to hold the iPod instead of turning it over to security, and that seemed to satisfy Josh's anxiety for the moment. The guard agreed and was satisfied that he had thoroughly performed his scan. We were escorted onto the elevator and delivered inside the locked-down psychiatric emergency department, also known as CPEP. To say I was naïve the first night I walked into the Comprehensive Psychiatric Emergency Program with my son is an understatement.

Having had some emergency room experience, I figured that we had several hours of waiting ahead of us and was glad I had the foresight to bring a cellphone charger and a notebook. What I didn't realize was that I should have brought comfy footwear, snacks, a blanket, and a book or two. We were in CPEP for a little more than seven hours. We did not speak with a single staff member (except to ask for aforementioned blankets, socks, and snacks) for almost five hours, but there wasn't more than two other patients waiting to be seen. What I didn't know then was this would be our shortest stay in the CPEP unit. There would be more visits to follow and even longer wait times before Josh would be assessed; our longest would be twenty-seven hours.

Josh's father met us at the hospital shortly after we arrived in CPEP. Since our divorce more than a decade before, we were often unable to find common ground, especially where the boys were involved. Our support and custody agreement had changed just a few years prior, after Aaron decided to move in with his father full-time. This change obligated me to be sole financial responsibility for Josh and his care. While I knew we would do our best to co-parent through this crisis, in the end the decisions and culpability were mine alone.

Josh was surprisingly calm once we settled into the CPEP waiting room. His pain and anger had subsided. I felt as though the whole experience had been a bad dream. I watched him sleeping in the chair and thought twice about packing up and taking him home, certain that the day's events had been a simple misunderstanding.

As I watched him, wondering how he could be sleeping in such an uncomfortable position, his body contorted to fit into an extra small waiting room chair, my mind wandered back to when he was young. Josh had always been a quiet kid, opting to play by himself with his trains or army men in a dirt pile for hours. It wasn't that he didn't have friends; in fact, Josh had a way about him that drew people to him. He had great friendships, but preferred his own company to spending time with others. Josh had been a happy child, and throughout his elementary school years he loved school and had flourished.

I watched Josh's chest rise and fall. I could hear his calm, peaceful, sleeping breath. I'd watched him sleep thousands of times, often standing in the doorway of his room in the middle of the night. There was something so precious about watching my children sleep. In that moment, I wondered where had that happy young boy gone.

In middle school, Josh had had his first girlfriend. She was a year older, and it was a relationship filled with what I considered typical teenage drama. I wasn't happy about him dating so young, but knew it was a right of passage that was going to happen sooner or later. The break-up was exceptionally hard on Josh. He found himself ostracized from his group of friends and was completely heartbroken by the experience.

Sitting in the psychiatric emergency room that night, I recalled how worried I had been at the time, not sure how I could possibly help Josh heal his broken heart. Later, I learned that Josh had thought about killing himself over that breakup. I wondered if I had known then, whether I could have done something different to ease him through such tough growing pains.

Shortly before 3 am, a nurse approached to let me know that it was time for Josh's psychological assessment. I was alone in the waiting room; his father had gone home a few hours earlier. I reached over and gently touched Josh's shoulder, trying not to startle him awake. "Wake up, kiddo," I said softly. Josh was still groggy from sleep as a social worker escorted us from the waiting room into a small conference room. Josh's mood immediately changed. My few moments of peace and calm disappeared as accusations began to fly, even before we sat down on identical plastic-covered chairs. The story that Josh told to the social worker was consistent to what Officer Martinez had shared with me just hours before. "There is too much fighting in our home," Josh began, "The fighting is making things worse." Josh continued, "I don't feel safe with myself." The fear crept into my body as I listened, this time firsthand to my son's chief complaints.

Two more assessments were conducted with Josh before 5 am; the first with the floor nurse and finally with the staff psychiatrist. Each time we were escorted from the waiting room to a different, yet similar conference room - same small-sized room, same plastic-covered chairs.

Josh's demeanor changed again as we were ushered into this next set of assessments. Instead of anger, he began to present himself in a calm and practical manner, especially when meeting with the psychiatrist.

Under a different set of circumstances, that change in behavior may have set off my internal alarm system, but by this point I was numb. The final assessment was concluded and the treatment team did not feel that Josh was a candidate for admission. This recommendation was based almost solely upon the fact that Josh's claim that he wanted to harm himself had changed during the night. Without the risk of self-injury or a plan for suicide, the hospital felt that there was no need to admit him and, just like that, we were free to go home.

Chapter 3

• • • •

J osh had a pretty good understanding of what he needed to say to be admitted into the inpatient ward and, in this case, what he needed to say so that he wasn't. I know that Christmas had a lot to do with his desire to delay an inpatient stay. I did not want him to be hospitalized over Christmas either, but I also wanted to ensure that he was getting the support he needed. When we were discharged from CPEP, I was given a referral for a program called Partial Hospitalization and told to call them in the morning. I felt a little better thinking that even though he had not been admitted, at least he would soon have some support. Since the next day was Christmas Eve, I was only able to leave a message and would have to wait until after the Christmas holiday before I could speak to someone live.

It was a yearly tradition that I hosted Christmas Eve for my family. Josh and Aaron alternated years between my home and their father's, and this particular Christmas Eve I was looking forward to having them join our celebration. Just prior to dinnertime, Josh called. "Mom, we won't be coming to dinner tonight." He said that he wasn't comfortable seeing everyone, especially after spending most of the night before in the hospital. "I understand, Josh," I responded, and then added "I haven't told anyone about what happened." He said that he just needed time away from our house, but he'd see me in the morning. I hung up the phone and stood frozen for a few moments. Christmas was my favorite holiday to celebrate with the boys, and I worked hard to make it extra special. I was disappointed and sad, but I knew that the rest of my family was ready to eat. So I took the ham out of the oven and chose to pretend that it was a happy holiday.

On the Monday after Christmas, I received a call from the Partial Hospitalization intake coordinator, a kind woman who informed me that there was a three-week waiting list for an initial evaluation into the program. I was bewildered and started to cry right there on the phone. I had had it in my mind that because we had the referral from the hospital, I'd make the call and my son would be in the program as early as the day after the holiday. I was hoping and praying for it, especially because he was still sharing that he did not feel safe and that he was concerned about his mental health. I agreed to be placed on the waiting list and hung up the phone, wondering what on earth would happen next.

As luck would have it, early the following morning the intake coordinator called back and said that there had been a cancellation. We had an hour to get to the appointment, and I wasn't going to miss it for anything. During the psychological assessment, I worked with the financial office of the hospital to ensure that my insurance would cover the cost. I had not even considered that the insurance wouldn't pay for the program. "Do you know that this hospital is considered out of network for your insurance?" the financial administrator asked. It turned out that there was not a hospital within 200 miles of us that was considered "in-network," so an exception would need to be approved by the insurance company prior to Josh starting the program. This apparently wasn't anything new for the financial office, and the administrator quickly provided me with paperwork to sign so that she could begin the process of obtaining approval.

The assessment itself went well. Josh qualified for the program and, with any luck, the insurance would agree to cover it. We were good to go. He would come to the hospital every morning by 7:30 am and would stay until 3:00 pm each day. We'd be responsible for transportation. The program worked directly with Josh's school to obtain schoolwork and projects in progress so that he would not fall behind. It all felt like a good direction. I felt like I was able to take a deep breath again, feeling like he would finally begin to get the support he needed. As we were walking out of the building, the financial administrator called my cell phone. "You are all set," she shared. "Josh can start the program as early as tomorrow."

My hope was that after he spent a couple of weeks attending the Partial Hospitalization program, Josh would stabilize and then be back to his routine. I was excited for things to return to normal. I would soon learn that things don't always play out as we hope, especially in a mental health crisis like this one was shaping up to be.

The following morning, Josh started the program. Partial Hospitalization was located in a remote wing of the hospital, in the Behavioral Health building. It had a small parking lot, made much smaller by growing piles of snow from an early winter storm. A security guard monitored the morning drop off, so Josh could walk himself into the building without me escorting him.

On Josh's second day in treatment, I received a call from his social worker, Nancy, requesting a meeting with me to discuss Josh's attendance. I was feeling hopeful about his treatment and looked forward to receiving an update on his progress and diagnosis. We agreed to meet at dismissal the following day.

Being in the waiting room as the day-program dismissal occurred was an adventure. Parents, caregivers and transport personnel squeezed into every nook and cranny of very small 12' x 15' space. As I looked around the room, I recognized the tired, worried expressions on many of the faces. I imagined that those expressions were a result of the same exhaustion and fear that had all but taken over my life. I wondered silently to myself about these caregivers. What were their stories? How long had they been supporting their child or loved one through crisis? Where were they going for support?

My thoughts were suddenly interrupted when the dismissal bell rang. The population in the waiting room mushroomed as the patients were released to their respective rides home. Somehow in the sea of faces and activity, I saw Nancy motion for me to follow. I pushed my way through the crowd and she escorted me through the locked door separating the waiting room from the administrative offices and patient treatment rooms. Directly inside the door were the patient lockers. Every morning, each program participant was required to turn over phones and music players in order to minimize distraction and discourage relationships outside of treatment. The program had a strict rule discouraging these relationships. As I walked past the lockers, I remembered Josh coming home the day before with names and phone numbers of his "hospital friends" written on his arm and hand. He wasn't going to let a few rules keep him from connecting with these new friends.

I'd been in Nancy's office once before, during Josh's evaluation. It was a long narrow room with a window at the far end facing the Behavioral Health parking lot. Glancing out the window, I could see the cars and transport vans navigating their way out of the small lot.

To prepare for this meeting, I had written down a list of questions I had regarding Josh's care and safety. How were his moods? Was he opening up in the group sessions? Had she heard back from the school about his work? Did she feel that he was going to harm himself? I was anxious to hear how he was doing and how I could help him get back on track.

I settled into the chair closest to Nancy's desk. "Are you aware that your behavioral health insurance is outsourced to a third-party service provider?" The question caught me off guard.

"No, I'm not sure I understand what that means." As I replied, I thought back to the meeting with the financial office a few days earlier. "The only concern the financial office expressed was that my insurance was considered out of network for this hospital," I shared.

Nancy explained that I needed to be aware that every few days, the behavioral health managed-services company, hired by my employer to control insurance costs, would be evaluating whether or not my son still required care.

At first I didn't understand. I started to offer possible meeting times when I could make myself available to sit down with this managed care provider and discuss the current status of Josh's crisis. "That's not how it works," Nancy advised me. There would be no discussion with this managed care provider; they only spoke directly with the attending physician. Josh's treatment duration would ultimately be decided by this service provider and not by his doctor or treatment team.

I stared back at Nancy, trying to process this surprising information. I suddenly realized there was a strong possibility Josh would not be able to stay in the treatment program as long as was medically necessary. Panic rose inside my body. My heart beat loudly in my chest.

"It doesn't matter if the insurance company pays for the treatment. I will pay out of pocket for whatever services Josh needs." I wasn't sure how I would actually find the money, but I wasn't going to let finances get in the way of Josh's care. I wondered how an insurance company could recommend discharging him from the program when he was sharing openly that he didn't feel safe, that he thought of killing himself regularly and at times that he had a plan to do so.

"There is no way I'm going to sit back and allow treatment to be discontinued when he clearly needs support and is at risk for killing himself," I stated. Not on my watch. No way.

Nancy assured me that Josh's care was not in question at that time, but it was important that I be aware of the possibility that things could change at any moment.

* * *

After a couple days, the early morning drive across town to "Partial" quickly felt like routine. Josh and I chatted about easy subjects, like the weather or updates on his friends. After a week, the conversations changed to focus on his "hospital family," the other teens he had met in the program. Most of the stories Josh shared were benign, but a few concerned me, especially when he shared information about who had attempted suicide and by what means or about which medications the collective group of teens had rated best and worst. I often drove in silence after these conversations, not wanting Josh to know how scared I was upon hearing this information.

During the first two weeks of the program, there were numerous family and treatment team meetings to further assess Josh's situation. I was glad that the insurance coverage concerns did not seem to be impacting Josh's care. Nancy had not mentioned another word about it, and I figured no news was good news.

Most of the meetings were conducted in Nancy's office or in the adjacent treatment room. Josh's father was often in attendance, though he frequently worked out of town. In those cases he would join over the phone. Updates on the daily activities, therapy and school progress were followed by an assessment of Josh's mental health and coping skills. Josh was acclimating well to the program. "He's been very open about his dislike of your rules and anger with you, Mom," Nancy shared towards the end of his first week of treatment. No surprise there; at least on that point, Josh was consistent.

Josh's mental health continued to yo-yo. One day he would appear to be happy and confident, the next he would be angry and depressed. As the days passed, his depression and anxiety became more noticeable and concerning. "It is early in his treatment," I told myself, "things will begin to improve."

By the second week of the program, I had hoped there would be a diagnosis, but Nancy explained that that would require outpatient psychiatric evaluation. Diagnostic services were not part of the Partial Hospitalization program. Even without a diagnosis, new medications had been prescribed for Josh: Prozac for depression, Hydroxyzine for anxiety and melatonin to help him sleep, all in an attempt to stabilize his symptoms. Yet, Josh's mental health continued to slip quickly.

The treatment team monitored the speed of his descent. Without threats to harm himself or others, the team would not recommend inpatient care. Josh was aware that things were not getting better, and one morning on the way into the hospital, Josh turned to me and said, "Mom, I'm really having a tough time holding it all together." That afternoon, sixteen days into the Partial Hospitalization program, Josh informed his treatment team that he felt suicidal.

Unfortunately, even with a recommendation from the attending physician overseeing Josh's care, there was no simple transfer from one program to another within Behavioral Health services. So, in order for Josh to be assessed for admission, we needed to start over with the Emergency Department and repeat the steps we'd walked only a few weeks before.

Chapter 4

• • • •

An armed security guard pushed Josh in a wheelchair as he escorted us to the ward. The path took us through the deepest bowels of the hospital. As we walked through a section of the hospital that felt long forgotten and had clearly missed a number of opportunities for upgrade and refurbishment with its dingy, beige walls and broken floor tiles, it felt as though we had stepped back in time. Yet, I felt a connection to this place, as if the lonely, long forgotten halls of the hospital were a metaphor for how I was feeling.

We had just spent twenty hours in CPEP during our second trip to the hospital in three weeks. I had no idea what to expect; in fact, Josh seemed to have more information than I did through his friends from "Partial" who had previously been hospitalized. All I knew was that I had to fill out the third full set of admission paperwork since we had entered the hospital earlier that day, just to initiate the move from CPEP to the psych ward. I'd later learn that there is separate admission paperwork for the emergency room, for CPEP, for transfer to psych, and also for admission to the psych ward. None of the packets I had previously completed transferred from department to department. It may seem that the act of completing paperwork multiple times would not be such a big issue, but it was to me. I felt like the only communication that was happening at this point was between my pen and me. I didn't want to waste time on forms, I wanted to hear what was next for Josh's care. Yet no one shared any information with me as I walked along with the guard transporting my son to the adolescent psych ward.

Josh had been much more agitated during this CPEP visit. The wait was so much longer than the previous one. Nearly 12 hours after we were checked in, we finally met with the first member of the assessment team - a social worker - to begin the process. Since Josh had been on a regimen of Hydroxyzine for his anxiety, he was able to request a dose while we waited; at least he was able to calm down and sleep. I had been awake for more than 30 hours, surviving on pure adrenalin. As we made our way to the ward, I stole several glances at Josh as he sat quietly in the wheelchair while the guard navigated the way. He looked confident and calm on the outside, yet I saw fear in his eyes. I prayed that this would be the turning point for him, that he would receive the support needed and we'd be on the road to recovery.

Upon arrival to the ward, I was taken into a "family" room, a large lounge that I later learned doubled as the patients' television and game room. A nurse greeted me with another full set of frustrating paperwork to fill out. At this point, I was exhausted and started to protest, but my reaction made Josh upset and angry. "What's your problem, Mom? Just fill out the paperwork!" he sneered. Recognizing how stressful this was for both of us, I decided the best course of action was to simply fill out the forms again; the last thing I wanted was to create more stress and further aggravate Josh's condition

From that point on, however, I realized that it was important for me to keep a separate log containing all of the information that the hospital continually requested, especially my son's developmental information. Having a list of developmental milestones -- like the age at which Josh first slept through the night, walked, and was potty trained— gathered together ahead of time would make the paperwork process a little easier. I found that most of this information could be obtained from his primary care doctor. Having this prepared ahead of time would eliminate some of the stress of the situation, should I need to repeat this process in the future.

That night, as I completed the last of the paperwork for admission while Josh sat silently glaring at me, still frustrated with my exhausted attempt to voice my displeasure with the process, the nurse told me I could go home. I was confused. "That's it?" I asked.

"Your son needs some time to settle in," she responded.

While I understood that it was important to let Josh settle in, I had yet to speak to anyone who could give me information on the next steps for him and for me. My head was spinning. "What now? What next? That's it, just leave?"

The nurse informed me that I could call and check on Josh in the morning. My confusion only further angered Josh and I realized that I just needed to leave and let him get settled. What I really wanted to do was wrap my arms around him and hold him on my lap, like when he was little and had a skinned knee. I wanted to be able to kiss his "boo-boo" and make it all better for him. I felt powerless.

As I walked out of the ward that night into the frozen January air, I was in disbelief. Numbness settled into my body. I couldn't accept the fact that I had to leave Josh there in the hospital. As I stood in the parking lot, looking back at the building, the hospital looked dark and ominous. I felt fear rise in my body. Panic. I realized I had been given no information advising me as to what would occur next. I was given no instructions, no literature to take home, and I wasn't even sure if a doctor or anyone else would call me in the morning or whether there was some action that I needed to take.

I was in disbelief about the whole situation. I kept wondering how this had happened, what I had missed. How it had escalated so quickly. Less than a month before, we'd celebrated Josh's birthday. On that special and joy-filled day, we had some great laughs and things had felt good, hopeful. Now here I was walking out of the hospital, out of the adolescent psychiatric ward. My head was spinning. I had no idea what to expect; had no idea what was next. I was heartbroken.

Chapter 5

• • • •

The roads were empty, long deserted by those who had "normal" lives. Driving down the highway through the towns that separated the hospital from my home, my brain was fully engaged in wanting to figure out how I could have prevented this crisis. "What the hell, God?" I yelled "What. The. Hell!" Then from a deep, dark place within me arose a scream so primal, so otherworldly, that when I finally let it all out, there was nothing left in me but silence. My mind felt like it was shutting down, unable to comprehend the magnitude of the situation and unwilling to accept what was happening.

My husband Pete, Josh's stepfather, was waiting at the door when I got home. "Are you okay, Amy?"

I could tell by the look on his face he already knew the answer. I wasn't okay and I wondered if I would ever be okay again. "I really need a hug," I finally answered. "I need a big hug."

We'd only been married for a few years prior to Josh's crisis, but Pete brought into the marriage a level of kindness and love that I had never before experienced. It wasn't all roses: there had been times when we were at different places on our paths, times when those differences threatened the cohesiveness of our relationship. We'd also had so many blessed times full of joy, friendship, companionship and laughter. For the first time in my life, I found a partner who was open and willing to learn, grow and experience this journey by my side whatever might come.

I was grateful to come home to his loving arms, and he let me sit in silence for a very long time. "Did Josh give you a break this time or was his story the same?" he asked.

"The story was the same, but this time the focus was on his suicidal thoughts. He said that he wanted to kill himself and that he had a plan," I shared.

Pete sat for several minutes in silence and then asked, "How the hell did we end up here?" It was, of course, a rhetorical question.

Sleep did not come easy for me that night. I tossed and turned for hours, replaying the events that led to this point in time. What had I missed? How could this be happening? What new drama would the morning bring? Somewhere in the early hours of the morning, I finally fell into a fitful sleep. I dreamt that I was drowning. I opened my mouth to scream for help, but no sound came out. I tried to scream again and again, but still there was no sound. Just before I woke, I felt myself slip under the dark water one final time.

Chapter 6

• • • •

I t didn't take long after Josh's admission to learn about the next steps for his care. An initial treatment team meeting, which included Josh's assigned psychiatrist, social worker, and nurse, occurred the next afternoon. It was held in the "family" room, where we'd been the night before for Josh's admission. Even in the light of day, the room felt stark and cold and not even the couch and television could make it feel like a real family room.

Josh sat on the couch between his father and stepmother, and he shared that he had something to say: "Mom, I am not coming back to your house after I'm discharged from here. I am going to live with Dad." He told me that I had let him down. My rules, my parenting style, my long list of flaws and faults, at least in his opinion, had caught up with me. I had watched my son descend into mental illness and then I had to bear the crushing weight of his rejection and blaming.

I was devastated. When I had left the hospital the night before, it hadn't even crossed my mind that this could be coming. Yet here was this bomb, dropped right in my lap. Perhaps there were small hints, even before this hospitalization, that he had wanted to move into his father's house. The more depressed and off-balance his moods had become, the more Josh shared with me his disdain for all things that I did, especially my annoying desire to keep an eye on him. I did ask a lot of questions. I wanted him to check in when he was out for the day and I didn't allow him to spend the weekend couch-hopping without a plan for where he was going to be and when. Yes, I was that parent. I couldn't help it. I loved him so much. I had hoped that somehow these rules would keep him safe and out of trouble, but even so, I knew that standing firm on them could put me in a situation where I could jeopardize my relationship with Josh. I had felt that it was worth the risk.

Josh stared at me, waiting for a response.

"I understand, Josh," I said. "You've made it clear that you were not happy at our house." What else could I say? Inside I was screaming in pain. I wanted to shout, "No, please don't, please don't leave!" But I had learned the hard way when Josh's older brother had moved out to live with his father just a few years before. That situation had been a terrible fight that dragged out in the courts. I decided that it was best to just let Josh go. I felt that I'd be vilified no matter my response.

I couldn't image how I had fallen so short as a mother. I attended every activity, teacher's conference and sporting event. I was Mom's Taxi for years. I fished homework out of bedrooms and replaced lost wrestling shoes, baseball gloves and soccer cleats on demand. And I regretted none of it. In fact, I considered myself incredibly lucky. I often thought how great it was to have so much time with my sons, time I could spend focusing on their individual needs.

It took me days to stop crying after Josh's big revelation. I was in mourning. I could not have imagined feeling more scared and devastated than I felt. I couldn't fathom my heart breaking more than it already had, and then like a sledgehammer had hit me out of the blue, my heart was shattered.

"Do you think we should make an appointment with our marriage counselor?" Pete recognized that I was in a crisis. "Maybe he can give us some insight into how to manage through this situation."

"I don't think it matters," was my only reply.

Pete recognized that not only did it matter, but that what I needed was some immediate intervention before I found myself in the hospital right along side Josh. I felt like a wounded animal. That primal scream welled up inside me again, but this time when I tried to let it out, no sound came. Just like my dream a couple nights before, I was slipping under the water. Slipping. Slipping.

Doctor O'Brien saw me the following day. As Pete walked me into his office that bright and sunny January afternoon, I noticed the physical and emotional toll this experience had taken on my body. I felt weary. My steps felt purposeful, they were physically moving me forward, but they were without meaning. The constant crying and the sleepless nights were catching up with me. The night prior, I went to see Josh during visiting hours. It had taken an enormous effort on my part to hold myself together. I wondered if he could tell that my own foundation was cracked and that water was pouring in.

Doctor O'Brien's face was gentle as he carefully and compassionately walked me through points and counterpoints of the situation.

"I am scared to death that something is going to happen when he is at his Dad's house," I shared with him. "What if he really tries to kill himself and I'm not there to help?" I was sobbing, deep choking sobs.

In the midst of my breakdown, Dr. O'Brien said, "What if, Amy, you just stop fighting?"

"Stop fighting?" I nearly choked on my words.

"Yes. What if you accept that this is out of your control and focus on what you can do to keep Josh as safe as possible right from where you are."

His questions got my attention. I had completely lost sight of the fact that just because Josh would not be living in my house, it didn't mean that I couldn't still take care of him, watch out for him and, most importantly, be there for him when he needed me. Something in me shifted, though the mourning would continue for days and weeks to come. I knew then that I could somehow find a way to keep moving forward, to be there as best I could for Josh no matter what difficulties might follow.

Chapter 7

• • • •

January 2011

He's been in the hospital for eight days. I'm doing the best I can to be there for Josh in every way possible. I am still mourning the loss I feel knowing that he won't be coming back to live at my house once he's released. I am still in shock. Some days I don't even know what I should be doing. Do I pretend that it doesn't hurt me? It's hard not to show my feelings. Sometimes when I visit, the tears just flow. Once or twice, Josh has said that it's not my fault, but I am guessing he was just trying to stop me from crying in front of him. I really don't want to break down like that. Josh needs me to be strong.

I'm writing about letting go. I just don't know any other way to process the unending sadness and pain I feel while watching my son going down this path. Perhaps by writing, I will somehow figure out who I am and what, if anything, I could have done to change this course. Maybe I can even figure out what I can do going forward to heal for myself and hopefully for Josh, too.

Right now, I have no idea. I thought that I knew who I was. Just a month ago, I was all about the role of Mom. I took this role very seriously. I loved to cook every night - or at least most nights - for the family. I made it a priority to have meals together and I put love and care into everything I made. I enjoyed and prided myself on the family time. There was a real hope that this time together would build our relationships stronger. I had this fantasy of all of us sharing meals and thoughts about our day. Willingly spending some quality time together.

Some meals were like this, but many more were not. Often, mealtimes were uncomfortably quiet, tense, and not much fun. It caused so much anxiety for all of us, and I often wondered if it was worth my efforts to try to bring the family together like this. Even so, I really loved doing it and held out hope that one day it would start to look like the family mealtime I had long been envisioning.

I am absolutely crushed that Josh has chosen to leave. I already miss our time together before school. On many mornings, he and I watched the news before the school bus arrived, his head in my lap, me not even wanting to breathe for fear that the magical moments would pass too quickly and be gone forever.

Thinking about this makes me miss my children when they were little; I remember how I held my breath so often in those sweet moments, wanting nothing more than for the time to last forever. One of my favorite things was reading to them before bed, telling them stories that may or may not have been on the pages of the book we were reading. I miss them climbing up in my lap, snuggling against me. Even thinking about this now pulls at my heartstrings. How can this be? How can it be that I will no longer have either of my children living with me?

My heart hurts. It hurts in a way that can only be described as deep longing and mourning. I wonder if some of this is natural for parents to feel as their children grow up and leave home to explore and journey on a path of their choosing. It's hard for me to say, but I suspect that many parents do feel like I am feeling now. The empty nest syndrome, they call it. Yet I feel like there was a loud crash and suddenly I've found myself with an empty nest, without the natural progression that often accompanies this milestone. In fact, I feel like I've lost my son twice during this crisis, once to mental illness and the second time in a true physical way as he leaves my home and begins to sever his relationship with me.

One thing that I know for sure is that I have put my whole self into being the best mom that I could be for both my children. Deep down I was determined to love them the way I felt I hadn't been when I was growing up. I thought that by giving them what I felt I didn't have, I'd somehow save them from the pain that I felt as a child.

Even as I write this, I know that my childhood was not horrible; not in the least. I have come to believe that many of us grow up feeling like we needed something different than what our parents or caregivers were able to give us. I don't believe that it was because my parents were neglectful or didn't love me. I know that they loved me very much; there was a lot of love in our home. Even with my own children, I know that I have loved them to the best of my capabilities. However, I can't help but think that perhaps it wasn't enough or at least it wasn't what they needed from me in the way that they needed it.

I've certainly had some time to think about this, ever since Aaron moved out a few years ago. I've tried hard to figure out what I could have done better for both my children. While I am definitely feeling quite a bit of self-blame over Josh's crisis, I've felt a lot of self-blame for years before that. I think in some ways having my Josh continue to live with me after Aaron moved out made me feel like maybe I hadn't completely screwed up my mothering duties. But now, I feel like a complete failure. My heart and head cannot comprehend how, in the midst of this crisis, my son would choose to not want to be cared for by me.

I feel like I have failed in my self-assigned charter for my children's lives. I've been racking my brain and coming up with all the ways I have failed them. And the list is long: I wasn't there enough, I didn't have as much patience or compassion as they needed, I pushed too hard, I didn't push hard enough, and on and on. In many ways, I cannot even breathe now as I write this. The pain is just so deep.

I wonder if I will ever recover.

Chapter 8

• • • •

The first hospitalization lasted sixteen days. Despite Josh's big announcement about moving in with his dad, my days were filled with visitations, treatment team meetings, and trying to keep up with my full-time job. Luckily, my position at work was flexible and I was able to keep up with the expectations even as I was reeling from weeks of ups and downs with Josh's mental health. Exhausted, I just kept plugging along, hopeful that the situation would soon begin to shift and healing could begin for everyone.

The weather that January had been colder than normal, and yet there was a part of me that was so numb, I hardly noticed. The sun didn't shine often in our city that winter and the stark, grey landscape perfectly matched my despair. Each day, after I pulled into the parking lot outside Josh's ward, I sat in the car and mentally prepared myself for the treatment team meeting or the visit that would follow.

On one particular day, as I sat alone in my car, watching wisps of snow blow across the street and into a partially constructed new hospital building, I felt more anxious than normal. I was heading into what could be Josh's last treatment team meeting. There had been discussion about discharge planning earlier in the week, and since I hadn't seen much change in Josh's symptoms, I was feeling conflicted. I wanted him to come home, even though that didn't mean my home, but I worried that he was still in a crisis.

The day before, while visiting the ward, I had a hallway conversation with one of the floor nurses. I was grateful that she took the time to answer my questions about the treatment protocol.

"Why hasn't there been any focus on therapy for Josh?" I had asked. I hadn't realized, until that conversation, that the sole purpose of the in-patient stay was to stabilize Josh's symptoms and get him back home and into a normal routine as soon as possible. I presumed that there would have been some level of therapy, as well, but the nurse explained that type of treatment was expected to happen with his private practice therapist. Since Josh had been seeing the same therapist for several years prior to his breakdown, I found it difficult to believe that suddenly that would be enough to keep him out of harm's way. I wondered if he'd made enough progress that he'd once again feel safe with himself. I wasn't so certain that was the case.

Walking into the hospital, my body was on autopilot. The crisis was all-consuming. Somehow I managed to navigate from the hospital lobby up to Josh's floor, and the next thing I knew, I was standing in front of the adolescent psych ward door.

Had I pushed the bell to be buzzed in? I couldn't recall, so I pushed it and looked through the window to see if the receptionist was at the desk. The desk was empty, but I could see patients and staff milling around. One of the nurses on staff noticed me standing there and came to open the door. "Hello, Ms. White," she said. "The last team meeting is running behind. Feel free to wait here by the door."

While waiting outside the "family" room for Josh's treatment team meeting to convene, my thoughts were still on his impending discharge. Adding to my increased anxiety was the fact that just days prior, Josh's girlfriend had ended their relationship. My heart broke when I heard that she'd delivered the message to him while he stood at the payphone in the middle of the ward's main hallway. Outwardly, Josh seemed to handle this news better than expected, but I wasn't convinced. I guessed that he didn't want anything to keep him from being discharged. I suspected that the pain of this breakup ran deeper than he was letting on, and it was likely we'd see this issue surface again in the future.

Once situated in the team meeting, the social worker kicked things off with an update on Josh's progress. "Josh appears to be managing things well, including the recent breakup," she advised. Those last words, I knew, were directed right at me. I had spoken to her privately, voicing my concerns over Josh's discharge planning and his safety after the breakup. It was a conversation that hadn't been well received.

"I haven't seen much change or improvement in Josh's symptoms," I responded.

The social worker had moved on to her next point in Josh's progress report, ignoring my response.

"I haven't seen much change or improvement in Josh's symptoms," I repeated a second time. It was not unusual for my input to be dismissed during these meetings. Josh's urgent desire to move to his father's house, along with the story of consistent turmoil and fighting, made me an easy scapegoat for Josh's breakdown. I noticed how, as his story unfolded, the treatment team members had shifted the way I was engaged in the process.

I felt that every aspect of my role as Josh's mother came under question. "Perhaps if you hadn't traveled so much for business when Josh was younger, he wouldn't be so angry with you now. Have you considered how impactful this must have been on him growing up?" I was asked by the social worker shortly after Josh's admission. What about all of the times that I had been there for Josh? Did they know how I had shifted my work and travel schedule to be home as much as possible, even if it meant leaving for business trips early in the morning or coming home late at night so that I could be there when he awoke? I was conflicted, wondering how to share my side of the story, which happened to be in sharp contrast to what Josh was sharing, without coming across defensive and as a result guilty. Unfortunately by then, the treatment team had all but stopped pursuing any other possible contributors to his breakdown.

I had expected some stigma to be associated with Josh's crisis, but I was caught completely off guard by the experience of being stigmatized by the very medical facility that was caring for him. Naively, I had thought that the treatment team members would be "wanting" to partner with me for the highest care of my son. What I found instead was that once they formed their opinion about Josh's situation and its probable cause, they stopped pursuing any other possible contributors to his breakdown. Given the goal to stabilize him as quickly as possible, believing there was no further excavation necessary on their part, they could then start to prescribe medication and some out-patient therapy, and Josh would be on his merry way.

* * *

Unfortunately, this feeling of being stigmatized would happen a number of times during Josh's crisis, but the first time really took me down to my knees. It caught me so off guard that I wasn't sure I could recover. While it was awful feeling blamed and attacked as a parent, as a mother, I was scared to death that Josh wouldn't get the care he needed because the treatment team had stopped looking for the cause of his breakdown.

When Josh first went into the hospital, I had willingly gone along with everything the team recommended, I supported their initial thoughts about how to stabilize his condition and what steps and protocol were necessary to create the treatment plans. Yet, some of the recommendations didn't feel right to me. In some cases, the recommendations, such as taking a wait-and-see approach, didn't feel strong enough and, in other cases, like when an increase or change in medication was recommended, the recommended protocol felt too much for the symptoms of depression, anxiety and suicidal ideation that Josh was presenting; yet I didn't speak up.

When I initially realized that the team was suspecting me to be the cause of Josh's crisis, I remained silent. I did not even know where to begin to explain or defend myself against the group consensus. It was partly because I was still in shock from witnessing Josh's rapid spiral into crisis, but there had been another reason.

I stayed silent because I was brought up with the belief that I should always respect my elders and that people in positions of authority, whether they were doctors, teachers or clergy, were never to be questioned. I had been taught that these individuals had absolute power. Abiding by this belief didn't always serve me. In fact, it hurt me in many ways.

When I gave someone absolute authority over a situation, in turn, I felt powerless. I had given my power away to the treatment team and I came face-to-face with this realization as I tried to determine how I could respond while maintaining my focus on what was in Josh's best interest. I knew I needed to change my deep-rooted belief to ensure Josh received the care that he required.

But, as in the past, I had stayed silent. I stayed silent when they began for formulate their opinions. I stayed silent when they blamed me for being a working mother, being too overbearing or not overbearing enough. My silence implied agreement and guilt to all involved -especially, I imagine, to Josh. I became the perfect scapegoat. I imagined the multi-disciplinary team report on Josh would sound something like this: "Of course, this poor young man has had a terrible mother all these years, and it's no wonder he is now no longer mentally stable."

I cannot pinpoint the exact moment when things changed, but I suddenly realized that all of the focus on Mom as the bad guy wasn't accomplishing what was truly important, and that was stabilizing and keeping Josh safe. While I had participated in my share of blaming myself, I knew I was not the cause of Josh's breakdown. I realized that

I needed to step in and break up the blame-fest so that he could have a chance to receive the real help he needed.

However, I knew that attempting to address the beliefs about me, as the bad parent and culprit, would do nothing to support Josh's care. I chose instead to allow the blame to continue to fly as it would, without the need to defend myself, and then I made it my sole role to ensure that Josh got the best possible care with the focus on the right treatment, whatever it took.

As a result of this decision, I could no longer remain silent. From that point forward, I did my best to speak up when I did not agree with a treatment protocol, a change in medication or dosage, or a discharge plan when it was clear that Josh was not ready to leave in-patient care. Initially, my change in behavior was met with a bit of passive patronizing and condescending pushback. I can't say I blamed them; I suspected they figured I'd give it a shot and then I'd go back to my silent self.

But it was right around this time that I had a really big realization. While these doctors had MD appended to their name, I had M.O.M. I realized that I was a specialist and an expert on my child; no one else could possibly know him the way that I did.

* * *

During our last treatment team meeting, Josh appeared calm and confident. He was given time to share his thoughts and feelings about his stay and his progress. "I feel ready to go home," he said. There was a notable difference during this team meeting. In many of the past meetings, Josh continued to repeat the story of how I had played a big role in his breakdown. In this meeting, though, he shared how he felt stronger and healthier than he had felt in months. His comments confirmed the team's recommendation that he was ready for discharge. I held my breath, hopeful that medical experts knew something that I didn't about my son's progress.

Chapter 9

• • • •

A t the time that Josh was discharged, he was still presenting symptoms of depression and anxiety, but was no longer experiencing suicidal ideation. Without the desire to harm himself or others, the treatment team felt he had stabilized enough to recommend the discharge. Josh was referred back to the Partial Hospitalization program as a way to transition him safely to his father's home. This time, they had an immediate opening for him to attend the program, and the transition happened smoothly.

Even though Josh was living with his father, I still saw him nearly every day, often while driving him to or from the program and during treatment team meetings. Our relationship was strained. We'd often sit in silence; the easy flow of our past conversations became a distant memory. Josh's view of my role in his breakdown continued to play front and center.

While I had come to the understanding that I did not cause his breakdown, it was hard not to look for all of the ways that I might have had a role in it. It was easy to turn the blame on myself, especially the longer this crisis continued. It also became increasingly difficult to find the strength each day to get out of bed and keep facing the scary reality of this situation. I felt so alone. I really didn't know what to do or where to go to find support for myself. It felt like everything was falling apart.

This wasn't the first time in my life I had experienced this feeling. As far back as I could remember, there were times when things felt like they were truly falling apart. As a young child, there was uncertainty and confusion in my life. Even before I recognized what was happening, things were hanging in the balance for me. I felt lost in the mix, caught between a home filled with sadness and crisis intermixed with what I always considered to be a "very Brady" upbringing.

There were several pivotal falling apart experiences for me, including my mother's prolonged postpartum depression and witnessing the exhaustion of my parents as they supported a child - my sibling - with severe attention deficit disorder. Maybe it was because I was the eldest or maybe I misinterpreted the signs and signals from my parents, but I felt as though I had done something wrong, something to cause the disharmony. I decided, at a young age, that it was my responsibility to fix or solve the crises in our family, because I believed that somehow I was directly responsible for the tough days we experienced.

As I got older, I continued to believe that when things went wrong, I was responsible. Because of this, I found myself in one difficult relationship after another with friends, boyfriends, and even mentors. Drama ensued. Things fell apart. I spent a great deal of time wondering what was wrong with me; each and every time, I found myself heartbroken and blaming myself. As long as I continued to act on this belief, things in my life fell apart over and over again for years.

I wanted to do it differently this time, to change the course of the pattern. I knew that taking on full responsibility and blame for Josh's crisis would not help him or me heal. I recognized that I needed to seek out support and guidance.

I was hoping to find support through a local group or agency. What I really wanted to find was some common ground, to know I was not alone; to feel as though there were others who understood what I was going through, to find people who could listen, lend advice or at least share their process, tools, and strategies with me. I was even okay with just finding someone willing to simply sit with me through the pain.

Yet, I had no idea where to start. I consulted with Dr. O'Brien, but he didn't have any recommendations or resources. I tried an Internet search, but that returned tens of thousands of results, and I was overwhelmed. I narrowed down my search terms and tried a number of different ways to research my options. After considerable searching, I found very little information.

After almost no luck finding local support, I recalled that the company I worked for had an Employee Assistance Program and I decided to give them a call. What came next truly surprised me. My conversation went something like this:

Me: *"I need information on support groups in my area."*

EAP: *"I can set up an appointment with a local therapist."*

Me: *"I don't need a therapist, I need to find a support group focused on dealing with mental health crises."*

EAP: *"Um, I can refer you to a therapist for 3 sessions."*

Me: *"Is there anything else you can offer? I don't need a therapist."*

EAP: *"What is it that you want?"*

This went round and round a few more times and finally, I said, "I don't know what I want; support, a group that can support me," to which the program representative responded that they couldn't help me. I was frustrated and exhausted. Up to this point, every road I went down to find support seemed to lead to a dead end.

I even reached out through my personal support circles, and a few times felt that I was close to finding someone I could talk with who understood what I was going through. Each time a possible contact was identified, the answer that came back was, "No." One response that truly drove home my understanding of why I was having such a challenge finding support came from an acupuncturist who was trying to help connect me with another of her clients. "I asked my client, who is having a similar experience to yours, if she would want to meet for coffee to talk, but she said no, she doesn't talk about her situation openly. In fact, even her close friends don't know." It was no wonder I was having such difficulties finding support; the stigma and secrecy around mental illness caused people to be afraid to share their experiences.

My path to finding support was so jagged and filled with potholes that I totally lost faith that I would find someone, anyone, who truly understood and was willing to share and support in the capacity that I felt I needed. In some ways, I still find this to be true.

Chapter 10

. . . .

The four weeks that had passed since Josh's last hospitalization were a blur. During two of those weeks, Josh had been part of the partial program again. He had a different social worker assigned to him, which meant the process started over again. I immediately set up time to meet with the new social worker, Charlie, so that we could review Josh's history, concerns, and symptoms. I didn't want to lose any time bringing the team up to speed. Josh was actually excited to be working with Charlie, and I'd soon learn that he was popular with many of the teens in the program. Learning this gave me an immediate sense of relief and hope for Josh's treatment.

That relief soon turned to disbelief. During the first meetings with Charlie, I felt immediately put on the defensive as he coached me on ways that I could better parent Josh so that he wouldn't be so angry with me.

"You know, Mrs. White, Josh is sixteen. Don't you think it's time that you give him more space?"

"More space? What does that even mean?"

"You know, relax his curfew and don't be so concerned with who he's with or where he's hanging out," Charlie responded. Clearly he and Josh had spoken at length already.

All I could do was stare at him in disbelief as his words sunk into my brain. I sat in silence in his long, narrow office. I was surprised and angry. I had expected to partner with this man to move Josh's treatment forward, and he had not even taken the time to get to know me. He knew nothing about my relationship with Josh prior to this crisis. How close we had been. How my heart broke over and over as that special relationship we had was disintegrating right before of my eyes.

Moments later, Josh joined the meeting. When he entered Charlie's office, he had a scowl on his face. I could tell he was angry. Even though I had seen him fired up before and I recognized it in that moment, I didn't expect the rage that followed. I felt like I'd been ambushed. Josh was screaming at me, raging against my rules and my perceived parental shortcomings. Based on the intensity of Josh's reaction, I realized that Josh and Charlie must have spoken shortly before I arrived. I cannot say how long the lambasting continued; it was likely only a few minutes, and during that time, there was no attempt on Charlie's part to bring it to an end.

Once the room was silent again, as if the verbal explosion had not even occurred, Charlie moved on to the next point of business. Even though the treatment team recognized that Josh's symptoms of depression and anxiety were heightened compared to his last partial-hospitalization, there was increased concern that the insurance would not continue to cover his care, especially since it was the second time he'd been in the partial program.

I told Charlie that I would not allow the insurance situation to obstruct the treatment that Josh needed. I had already made the decision a few weeks prior. I reiterated my intent to do whatever was necessary to ensure that Josh got the treatment that he needed.

Charlie stared at me for a moment and then reached into his file cabinet and produced a self-pay form. I guess he wanted to call my bluff, to prove that I wasn't in fact standing behind my son as I had claimed. I may never forget the look on his face as I began, without missing a beat, to complete the self-pay paperwork. I wasn't joking. I was prepared to lose it all and more if that was what it took to ensure that Josh was safe and that he was getting the help that he needed; little did I know how often this resilience was going to be put to the test.

Chapter 11

• • • •

February 2011

Josh was discharged from partial hospitalization this month, and I've been holding my breath. He started at school in his father's district, and I've already spoken to the guidance counselor to make sure that I understand his schedule and also the plan should something start to stress him out. I was able to get permission from the school to allow for some medication to be held at the nurse's office, just in case. Having him out of the hospital setting but not in my home is both heartbreaking and anxiety provoking. I know that I cannot stop him from harming himself or quickly escalating into rage or depression, but having eyes on him makes me feel like I'd be able to respond quickly if I were to see things begin to change. Now, I am notified by a phone call. I have begun to have panic attacks every time my phone rings. Unfortunately, in my job I am on the phone often and receive phone calls all day long. However, it's those calls late at night that truly send fear through my system, even before I answer the phone. I am exhausted and my nervous system is fried.

I don't know what I was expecting, but this is not it. I guess I really thought that Josh would receive the support he needed while in the hospital so that he could begin to heal. Instead, it seems like the responsibility to get him the support he needs falls squarely on the parents and not the treatment team. So while he was in a safe place to begin to pull back some deep layers of his personal story while in-patient, I'm now driving him to a 50-minute therapy session twice a week, which acts as nothing more than a ripping off of the Band-Aid. Then I pick him back up.

The fallout from these therapy sessions has been brutal. He often comes out of the sessions angry or fired up about what has been wrong in his life, most which has somehow been caused directly by me. I am in deep fear at this point; not for my safety, but for his. I cannot understand how it makes sense that he should be attempting to do this therapeutic work without so much as a safety net. I do my best to provide that net, but he is not with me fulltime now and while I do what I can to provide him with support, I feel sorely unqualified to help him.

This weighs heavily on my heart. The longer he is in this place, the more deeply I am going inward to blame and shame myself for all the ways that I may have contributed to it. My heart knows that I have done the best I could as a parent; my mind is not so sure.

There isn't much time to play the blame game with myself right now. Two days ago, we ended up back in the CPEP waiting room. This time because Josh chose to use a hunting knife to carve up his arm while at his father's house. He didn't feel safe with himself, and I knew even before we saw a staff member some ten hours after we arrived that he would not be going home that day.

I don't know how to help him. I don't know how to help myself. The further down this road we go, the scarier and more life-threatening this experience feels. I'm lost. In many ways, I feel just as lost as my son right now.

Chapter 12

• • • •

The second in-patient hospitalization began the same as the first, from the long wait in CPEP to the guard-escorted walk through the bowels of the hospital. By the time Josh was settled into his new room in the adolescent psych ward, I was exhausted and my nervous system was on edge. Before I drove home that night, I sat in my car and cried for almost an hour. Even though I had been in that same parking lot and same hospital ward just a few weeks before, as I looked up at the window where I knew my son was resting, my heart broke in a whole new way.

This time there was a physical injury that needed to be addressed, as well. Josh had used the hunting knife to carve a word on his bicep. Each letter was several inches high and wide. This felt like a serious cry out for help. I'd later learn that Josh had heard a song that reminded him of his ex-girlfriend, and that led to him cutting up his arm. It truly scared me. Josh had recently shared, after encouragement from his outpatient therapist, that he had started cutting as a way to cope with his pain. My deepest worry had been that he would severely hurt himself and that it would happen when he didn't have anyone around to help him.

There was a part of me that truly understood what he was feeling from the standpoint of wanting the pain to go away and wanting to feel the pain at the same time. I wanted his pain to go away; I wanted my pain to go away, too. My heart broke to see Josh struggling. I was exhausted from the emotional rollercoaster ride and terrified that there was no end in sight. As I drove home from the hospital that night, the only thing I knew for sure was that somehow I needed to get a good night's sleep because the cycle of meetings, care planning, and hospital visits were going to start again first thing the next morning.

Somewhere in the middle of a dark, stressful dream, a phone was ringing. Slowly, as it continued to ring, I began to realize that it was my phone. The panic rose in my body as I reached for it and answered. It was Josh's newly assigned social worker calling to give me an update. It was first thing in the morning and she reported that Josh had had an uneventful night, had eaten his breakfast and taken his medication without issue. What a relief. An introductory team meeting was scheduled for that afternoon. The social worker explained that Josh would have a new treatment team, completely different from the first hospitalization. As the fog cleared from my head, I began to realize that this meant we'd be starting from square one with his treatment again. The lack of consistency was frustrating and scary.

As I drove towards the hospital that afternoon in the middle of a snowstorm, I was mentally prepared for another round of treatment team introductions, and braced myself for Josh's input on how badly I had let him down. I was so lost in my thoughts, I hardly remember driving. As I parked my car in what had become a familiar spot outside the Behavioral Health Services building, I felt as though my entire world was spinning out of control.

Sitting in the "family" room once again, I found myself retelling Josh's story from the beginning, replaying the list of symptoms and concerns and rehashing the experiences that led to this visit to the adolescent psych ward. Josh was much more agitated this time. His anger was no longer directed at me alone; the individual treatment team members were also fair game. Since he had already spent more than two weeks in this unit, he immediately made his grievances known, pushing back on some of the rules and regulations that he would be required to follow as a patient. The lack of privacy, strict rules about personal relationships and limited phone time were among his chief complaints.

His anger was now showing up in a flash. The change in his behavior had been marked since his first hospitalization. There was no warning before it hit the "red zone." When it did, he punched walls, threw chairs and raised his voice. Given Josh's athletic physique, it was intimidating to be on the receiving end of such rage. It often intimidated me. He never physically injured anyone while enraged, though many inanimate objects met an early end to their useful life while in his presence.

Josh's anger and oppositional mood swings escalated at the same speed that our relationship deteriorated. When I showed up for the daily visiting hours, Josh often turned me away, letting me know that he did not want to see me that day. Each time I arrived for a visit, I held my breath while I waited to be buzzed into the ward. I never knew if I'd get a chance to see him or be turned away before I finished signing in.

Many times when I arrived, Josh would be in the "family" room. By late afternoon, the room had been transformed from a family conference room to a patient recreation room. One of the nurses on staff would go in and ask Josh if he wanted to see me. Some days he asked me to wait a few minutes. Other days, he came right out and let me know he didn't feel like visiting with me.

It was difficult to hear these words, though there was a part of me that was proud to witness him confidently stating what he needed and wanted. As much as it hurt me to know that I wouldn't have the alone time with Josh that I was hoping for, I would not force him to see me out of obligation. Instead, I allowed him the space to choose what he wanted and needed in those moments.

Usually, I showed up with some little treat for him: a cupcake, a cheeseburger, or a new notebook and pens. Even when I was asked to leave, I gave him these gifts and felt better to know that he had some comforts of home even while he was in the locked hospital ward.

Once in a while, as I walked back to my car, I could see him sitting in the window of his room. I wondered if he was watching me or was just lost in his thoughts, daydreaming about better days.

Chapter 13

• • • •

March 2011

The latest hospitalization lasted eleven days. Josh's arm is healing well as far as I've been told. He won't let me see it. I've been concerned about infection, and it's difficult for me to trust that all is well. I just want to make sure that it doesn't need attention, but Josh is adamant that he doesn't want me to see it. I am so grateful that he didn't cut too deep; my greatest fear is that he will do something to harm himself and unintentionally end up killing himself.

Even though he's out of the hospital, I do not feel confident that anything will change. There has been no formal evaluation or assessment, and there's no diagnosis. Josh is being treated for symptoms of depression and anxiety. This was what they have been treating him for since his first partial hospitalization, but there are no concrete answers as to what he is experiencing or what may be causing his change in behavior. The cycle has been repeating like a bad nightmare. After each discharge, he seems to be more stable and more hopeful about his progress. The hospitalizations seem to give him a chance to rest and take a break from the noise that has taken over his thinking, but the stabilization doesn't last very long. I just cannot believe that there isn't something more available for him to help him on the path to recovery. He is either in inpatient care or he's out on his own working with a therapist for 50 minutes once or twice a week. There's *nothing here that appears to be setting him up for a successful recovery, at least not that I have witnessed so far.*

I am exhausted. This process has taken a toll on me. I haven't felt well for a very long time. I don't wake up rested, even when I sleep through the night. I have days where I feel really strong and grounded, and days where I just want to climb back in bed and cry. In fact, the longer Josh stays in crisis, the more I'm finding that I am taking on the responsibility for his pain. I know that I didn't cause this situation, but my brain is intent on showing me all of the ways that I let Josh down over the years. These thoughts haunt me; I find that I cannot escape the pain of realizing how I could have done things differently and better for him and for Aaron, as well.

I know that I need to stay out of the place of beating myself up here. I know that this will not help with Josh's healing. I am so far outside my element right now. I don't know what to do or how to help him, and I don't know how to help myself move forward in a loving way. I know I am not responsible and yet, here I am, as I have often done over the years, allowing myself to fully own the whole situation.

It's time for me to make a change, but I don't even know how to begin. I feel so alone and scared. Stuck in the grip of fear. Afraid that I will make things worse and that Josh will end up killing himself while I'm trying to figure out how best to support him. To make matters worse, there was no transition to the partial hospitalization program when Josh was discharged this time. I was told that it was because he'd already participated in the program twice. I'm sure it has to do with my insurance provider, but regardless, he left the hospital and went right home to his father's house and then right back into school. We are a few days in and so far so good. I know that I will be holding my breath for some days still to come.

Chapter 14

• • • •

After Josh's second discharge, I realized that my situation wasn't just going to go away and that things were not going to return to normal. I didn't even know what normal was anymore, but I knew that my new "normal" wouldn't look anything like what it had before his crisis. I also realized that camping out in my blanket cave, not eating well and hardly sleeping was taking a physical and emotional toll on my life and that it wasn't the way to help my son.

I needed something that would get my butt in gear and get me started on a path of self-care. I had thought about taking up running, Zumba, or going back to the pottery studio where I had been taking classes during the year prior to the crisis. Nothing sounded good to me. It was exhausting to even think about getting myself up and out. I was conflicted because my days revolved around ensuring that Josh was okay, visiting him in the hospital, attending family meetings, school meetings and doctors' appointments. I made up excuses that I didn't have time. I didn't have the energy.

In a way, I was punishing myself. There was a part of me that didn't feel as though I deserved to take care of myself. Clearly, I hadn't been able to take care of my son. I felt like I had failed. Being an active parent for my children and doing the best I could for them was always my top priority. In fact, it was more than that; it was how I defined myself as a "good" parent. Evidently, given the circumstances, I had missed that mark completely.

One day, I realized that just because my experiences weren't happening the way I had imagined, it didn't mean it was the end of the world. It meant only that I needed to adjust my expectations. In fact, even more, it meant that I needed to let them go completely. The energy spent struggling to "understand" where things had gone wrong was really best spent supporting what was happening with Josh in the moment. It was a big shift, like a moment of setting myself free - free to allow the unfolding of what I was experiencing with my son. Free to allow life to take the twists and turns it needed to take.

By releasing my expectations, I found that I was less impacted by the crises that arose. So much of my initial reactions had been wrapped up in the "should have" and "shouldn't have" mentality. The bottom line was that I didn't want this to be happening to Josh; I didn't want it to be happening to me. Accepting that it was happening and that it wasn't "off track" was a true gift. It felt as though this was the beginning of acceptance for me.

I knew that I needed to address the immediate things that were not working for me. I was living in constant fear. I was hiding from life and not treating myself well at all. I started asking around to see if I could find something that would get me out of my funk and get me back to living my life again. It was then that I was told about a yoga program being offered by a local studio called "40 days to Personal Revolution." I signed up immediately.

The program included a commitment to practice yoga six times a week, participate in weekly workshops, and focus on mediation, journaling and improving diet. This was absolutely perfect for me. Once I committed, I was dedicated to participating full-on. The intensity of the program mirrored the intensity of what I was experiencing while attempting to come to terms with Josh's illness and the physical, mental, and emotional strength I needed to have to support him. It created balance.

During this same timeframe, I looked for other ways to ease my emotional pain. I had been doing quite a bit to honor myself with the almost daily yoga and, while it served my need for intense activity, I couldn't help but feel as though I needed something even more intense - and perhaps even something painful - to counter my pain.

I chose to go the route of a tattoo, a half sleeve designed around the Hindu deity Ganesh. Ganesh is the elephant-headed god known as the remover of obstacles, as well as the lord of beginnings, patron of arts and science, and deva of intellect and wisdom. While my connection to Ganesh was not religious, it was most definitely spiritual. I felt that the symbolism and meaning behind his story matched my situation perfectly, and the tattoo suited what I was trying to accomplish. It became a reminder of my strength and courage, and that often out of pain comes something very beautiful.

Chapter 15

• • • •

April 2011

It's been a very stressful few weeks since Josh's discharge. It's hard to tell how Josh is really feeling. He says he's fine. He says he just wants to live a normal life. There are days when he really seems like he is fine. I start to exhale a little more, feeling like maybe I can begin to trust that things are on the upswing. But yesterday Josh had an incident in school. He says he was feeling overwhelmed and resorted to self-injury to manage the stress. Unfortunately, the school doesn't feel comfortable having Josh in their mainstream program given the risk and liability on their end. They are going to assign him a tutor after the spring break holiday. With any luck, he will still be able to finish off this school year.

I'm spent. One minute he is doing well, and the next everything blows up again. Can't he catch a break? Can't any of us catch a break?

I feel like this is happening to me as much as it's happening to Josh. I am sitting next to him on this Mr. Toad's Wild Ride and neither of us can find the stop button. So the ride just keeps going, twisting and turning, up and down with no end in sight. Writing this makes me feel a bit overdramatic, but as I look at the past four months, I cannot think of a better way to describe the hell I've experienced while watching helplessly as Josh's health continues to decline.

This disease that has taken over Josh's mind is a trickster. One minute he feels good, clear and strong. His amazing laugh is back. That smile and that gentle-souled young man are back. It's hard in those moments not to be fooled into thinking that we've turned the corner, that these are the first steps toward Josh returning to mental wellness; then everything turns on end. Suddenly, Josh is transformed into someone else all together. No matter how many times I witness this sudden metamorphosis, it still takes me by surprise. It crushes my heart just a little more. My faith lies in pieces on the floor.

I just dropped Josh at his father's house after his appointment with his psychiatrist. It was just by luck that he had a medication check up today. Given his lack of impulse control as evidenced by the incident in school, the doctor is recommending that his medication be adjusted. She changed the Effexor dosage, which replaced the Prozac during this last hospitalization, and added Abilify, an anti-psychotic drug said to boost the effectiveness of the anti-depressant. The doctor is still trying to stabilize Josh, yet even with the additions and changes in his medication, things are not improving. In fact, if I'm honest with myself, I know that they are getting worse. I don't know what to do or how to help Josh heal. I'm just numb.

Next week is spring break from school. Josh and I have been talking about going on a college visit. He's been interested in Annapolis Naval Academy. The timing feels right to get out of town for a few days; hopefully a change of venue will help improve Josh's overall health, and having a goal to work towards may be just what he needs to get back on track. He asked me today, on the ride home from his doctor's appointment, if his cousin could join us on the trip. I think it sounds like a great idea, and I'm looking forward to a few days away with both of them.

Chapter 16

. . . .

Winter turned to spring. I was surprised by the change. "When did this happen?" I thought time and again as I saw the budding daffodils and tulips coming up in my yard. It just wasn't something that I had given much attention, with my focus being so intensely on Josh.

As the weather warmed and the trees and flowers bloomed, Josh's moods were much more stable, and he seemed to be feeling better overall. The spring break trip with his cousin ended up being just what we needed. It felt like old times. Josh had been happy and excited for the adventure. The change of his medication definitely made him more tired than normal, but even so, we had lots of laughs and an easy time together. When we ended up touring the academy grounds in the rain, no one seemed to mind. It was such a contrast to our experience over the past months, I felt as though the whole episode had been a bad dream.

After walking through the Washington Mall, we stopped just before entering the Smithsonian National Air and Space Museum so that I could get a photo of the two of us. It was a great way to cap off our trip, exploring Washington's amazing museums and monuments. The photo we took together outside the museum sits on my shelf, a reminder of the special moment we shared.

Back at home, it felt safe to let my guard down and exhale. Josh was working with a tutor and though he'd lost the motivation and excitement he'd had after returning from the naval academy visit, he was putting in some effort towards his schoolwork. I knew with a little help and encouragement he'd be able to finish off the school year and put it behind him.

"I'd like to work at the camp again this summer, Mom," Josh mentioned as we chatted on the phone one afternoon shortly after our return from the naval academy. I hadn't even considered this as an option.

"Do you feel up for it, Josh?" Of course what I really meant was, "Are you sure that you will be safe enough to spend the whole summer living in the woods?" The camp was four hours from our house. I didn't want to discourage him from this idea; in fact, I was relieved that he was thinking about future plans. The psychiatrist had recently coached me that plans for the future were a good indication that he wasn't thinking of self-harming.

Josh had worked at the same camp for the better part of the previous three summers, and the joy it had brought him was undeniable. I still wondered if this would be too much, too soon. "Let's talk it over with your dad and your doctors and see if they approve of the idea." I suggested. Josh agreed.

The deadline for applying to be a camp counselor had passed, but the camp director was excited that Josh wanted to come back again that year and had an open position that would be perfect for him. I was excited about the possibility that Josh would be doing something normal and routine over the summer. Things felt like they were falling into place and moving in the right direction for all of us.

Both the therapist and psychiatrist agreed that this was a positive indicator in Josh's progress and, since the experience had proved to be good for his self-esteem and sense of accomplishment in the past, the hope was that this would be another step in Josh's healing process. Josh just had to pass his school year and have a meeting with the psychiatrist prior to his departure.

∗ ∗ ∗

As things began to settle down with Josh, I found that I had time to stop and look around at the parts of my life that I knew were lying in shambles around me. When Josh went into crisis, he became my only priority. Even though I worked diligently to keep my friendships, marriage, and work relationships afloat, there was only so much of me to go around. I needed to make some tough choices. My first choice was to keep trying to balance the spinning dishes on the top of the broomsticks that I was balancing on the blades of the chainsaws I was juggling. Balance. Spin. Juggle. Though I chose not to see it at first, it would only be a matter of time before the whole scenario came crashing down around me.

For the first time in months, I looked around to see how many "plates" I had dropped while my attention was focused squarely on Josh.

It didn't surprise me to find that some of my relationships were strained. Even when things in my life were calm, relationships had never been my forte. In fact, for much of my life I felt like a misfit when it came to figuring out how to be in a relationship. I wasn't very good at it. As a young child, I wanted to be liked and to fit in so much that I often lost myself early in a new friendship. I felt so socially awkward that I took cues from the friend or friends and acted as best I could to be just like them. I thought this would make them like me more. When the friendships didn't play out as I expected, I was left trying to figure out what I had done wrong and what I could do to contort myself into someone who was liked by other people.

Josh's breakdown left no room to twist myself into knots to please others. I felt the pressure on my marriage the most, though we had Dr. O'Brien and he really helped us hold things together when everything else was falling apart. The constant stress, worry and fear pushed Pete and I towards our breaking point. Most, but not all, of my close friendships sustained. I looked forward to the summer and time to heal and regroup and to begin once again to enjoy the time with my husband and friends in my life.

The school year came to a close, and Josh got by with a single grade-point average separating passing and failure. I was so glad he made it over the threshold and that all of his summer plans could be put into motion. In fact, Josh had been so certain he'd pass the school year and be working at the camp, his footlocker was all but filled. The last thing we needed to do was to meet with his psychiatrist for a final medication check and get her blessing, and we'd be on our way to camp.

While we drove to the doctor's appointment, Josh was filled with anticipation. "How long do you think this appointment will take? Do you think we could stop for socks and a belt on the way home?"

I looked over at his face as he awaited my answers, and for the first time in what felt like years, I saw a sparkle in his eyes and a true smile on his face. "We are making the right decision," I thought to myself. "This summer is going to bring him back to life." My guard was completely down. We'd made it through hell and back. I was relieved and grateful that we had survived.

We arrived at the appointment a few minutes early and sat in the car to finish listening to a new song Josh wanted me to hear. We walked into the office just as the doctor was making her way out to the waiting room to collect us, and we were directed down a long hallway. Her office was located in a small office building that skirted a greenway. Often when we were there, deer and woodpeckers were visible outside her window. That day, the woods were empty, but the lush green of the vegetation was breathtaking. We took our seats, Josh on the couch and me in a chair. It was a comfortable arrangement that allowed Josh to have the center of attention on him, where it belonged. The doctor joined us, facing Josh.

"How are you feeling?"

"I'm doing great!"

"Have you had any thoughts about self-harm?"

"None. I haven't cut in weeks, either." He was proud of that fact.

"That is great, Josh, sounds like things are going really well."

Josh's face lit up with a huge smile. "They are and I'm really glad that I am feeling so much better." The appointment was all but over at this point; we just needed her final approval and Josh would be on his way to camp in just a few days.

Suddenly, the energy in the room changed. Josh had a serious look on his face. I caught my breath wondering, "What just happened?"

"I want to stop taking the Abilify," Josh announced. I felt like my brain couldn't process what he was saying. He hadn't mentioned this to me during our drive.

"Josh," I responded, "things are going so well, why would you want to make a change?"

Josh shot me a look that was meant to tell me to shut up. He continued, "I feel like a total zombie on this medication and I've gained a ton of weight."

I stared expectantly at the doctor. "Please," I thought, "please don't agree with him." I didn't want Josh on so much medication either, but things had been going so well and he was about to leave home for the entire summer. Four hours away. Living in the woods.

The silence in the room was deafening. Josh stared intently at his doctor, and she took a few moments to process this new information. My brain felt as though it might explode.

Finally, she began. "I completely understand, Josh." What? She did? Had she forgotten how bad things had been just a month before?

"I am willing to support you in eliminating the Abilify," she continued. I wanted to scream and openly disagree with her decision, but I sat quietly, knowing that forcing the issue wouldn't change what had just come undone. It was settled.

As we walked out of the office, Josh made a promise that if he started to feel off balance he'd let me know, and we'd get him back on the Abilify. I knew that it wouldn't be that easy.

Chapter 17

• • • •

J uly 2011

This month has been an emotional rollercoaster. The morning Pete and I took Josh to camp was stressful. As we were getting ready to leave the house, he was acting agitated because he wanted a chance to say good-bye to his girlfriend one more time. Josh's been dating her for a few months now, ever since he met her in his last in-patient stay. They denied the relationship for a couple months, but I'd found out afterward that she was part of the reason that he'd been so angry about the "no personal relationships" rule. She lives 20 minutes in the opposite direction of the camp and I argued that we needed to get on the road to be there by check-in time. After a relentless assault about why it was so difficult to do this one more thing for him, I ended up giving in and agreed to make the detour.

The rest of the drive was uneventful, and though I had been a bit apprehensive about dropping him off to work for the summer, I was still holding onto the belief that it would be a great opportunity. I hoped that it would be just what he needed to get himself back on track. I love how much he enjoys the work, and that makes it so much easier to support. Each summer I worry about him, but this summer in particular I was both worried and anxious, especially since he decided to stop taking one of his medications. It took a lot of trust for me to drop him off this year, but still, I couldn't shake the worry that sat right in the pit of my stomach.

I know that I cannot stop Josh from living his life and, as much as I'd like to, I can't protect him every moment. But whether he's at my house or not, I can do my best to make sure he's as safe as possible. Before leaving Josh at camp, I spoke with the director and let him know a little about the situation so that there could be additional eyes on him. I also shared a letter from his doctor outlining some high-level information about his situation. I asked that it be in Josh's file just in case.

Pete and I left Josh at camp and drove an hour further north to spend a few days reconnecting. The past six months has taken its toll on our relationship. I cannot imagine how difficult this experience has been on him. This crisis has been all consuming for me. I don't know how to balance our relationship when my primary focus is on Josh's care and keeping myself well enough to be there for Josh's needs. I am glad we decided to take this mini-vacation, though. We both felt that this time together was positive and healing.

During his first week, Josh received an award for being a favorite camp counselor. I was thrilled. To me, it indicated that he was doing and feeling well. Excitedly, I planned to make the trip to visit him the weekend after next. One of my favorite things to do while Josh is at camp is to treat him to a steak dinner. After he's been eating camp food for a few weeks, it fills my heart with joy to see him eating a good meal and getting a solid night's sleep in a real bed.

As I think of this, I remember back a couple of summers ago when it rained and stormed for the first two weeks of camp. Josh called me on a Friday night and asked me to please come up the next day and take him somewhere warm and dry. I hadn't planned to visit him that soon, but I knew that if he was asking for that favor, he really needed it. When I arrived, he was soaked to the bone. Everything he brought with him was wet and cold. I was lucky to find a room on such short notice and, after a quick slice of pizza, Josh climbed in bed and slept for almost 15 hours. Even though I sat in the hotel room and read magazines for the weekend, my heart was so full of gratitude that I was able to give Josh a little break.

This trip was different. Just days before I was planning to head up to camp to spring Josh for a few days, things became contentious. Josh was missing his girlfriend and, instead of the visit we'd planned, he wanted me to drive up to the camp, pick him up and bring him home for an overnight. He only had 24 hours' break each weekend, so the turnaround would have been nearly immediate. I understand how hard it is to miss someone like that, but I didn't think that I'd physically be able to handle the trip. It would be eight hours round-trip one day and then again the next. Josh was furious. He got angry with me because I didn't agree to his plan, and then he'd hung up on me. A few hours later, he called back with another proposal, asking me to bring his girlfriend up with us when we came to visit. The whole situation was nerve-wracking and the more I said no, the angrier Josh got.

I worried that instead of the fun visit I'd been hoping for, I may have to be prepared to bring him home. The night before I was planning to leave, I asked Josh if he still wanted visitors. Angrily, he agreed to stay with the plan. My stomach was in my throat for the entire drive up to the camp. I wondered, even though he agreed to the visit, if he would even see me, let alone decide to spend the overnight.

While the visit started off a bit uncertain, within a few hours he had relaxed and we were able to enjoy a wonderful weekend together. Before I dropped him back at camp, his mood shifted more negatively again. When I asked him why, he said because he was sure his boss was going to fire him. When pressed for details, he wouldn't share specifics. The information I received from his boss was not consistent with Josh's concern. Not sure what to believe, I hoped and prayed that he would continue to find his center and enjoy the rest of the summer working there.

That was not the case. His moods and his stability continued to spiral downward. I received calls from him screaming at me, demanding that I do this or that, threatening to quit his job if I didn't comply. Then he'd hang up on me when I didn't give him the response he wanted. I was sick with worry and unsure what to do. I contacted the on-site nurse, who told me that he seemed to be doing well and participated each day; they hadn't seen a major shift in his mood or indications that he was having any challenges. This concerned me even more. At least he was able to negotiate a week's vacation, and he decided to spend it with his father. I figured that it would be a good time to see how he was really doing.

The visit home did not start out well. Unbeknownst to me, Aaron drove up to the camp to pick Josh up for his weeklong stay at his dad's house. On the way home, they had a huge fight that ended with Josh being dropped off here instead of his father's, his travel bag and laptop thrown out onto the lawn. Josh was so mad that he smashed his cellphone into pieces. It was an absolutely ridiculous set of circumstances and yet, it was telling. I had to admit that things were not going well, as much as I willed him to be okay.

Things eventually settled down, and a couple hours later his father came to pick him up and took him home. From what I was told, Josh ended up having a good visit. There were no further problems - at least none that I knew about. I still didn't have a good feeling about him going back up to the camp for the rest of the summer. A few days before Josh was to return to camp, I offered to talk with the camp director, giving Josh an out so he didn't have to go back. But he really wanted to go. He said that he was feeling much better after his week at his dad's house, and that he was energized and ready to head back up for the duration of the summer.

What else could I do? I brought him back to camp.

Twenty-four hours later, I was on my way back to get him. He had had a major meltdown soon after his return to camp and quit his job. I called the camp director on the drive and found out that these meltdowns had been happening for a couple weeks. Everyone had hoped that the week vacation would be enough to stabilize the situation, but we all had to admit that it had not. I hung up with the director and had to pull over; my stomach felt like it was in my throat. I couldn't understand why the camp hadn't let me know that things had gotten so challenging, especially since I was on the phone with them weekly to check in. I'm not blaming the camp staff or the director; I am blaming myself for choosing to send him back when I knew he wasn't healthy. I wanted so badly for him to be well, for this summer to be the turning point for him. I had expectations, dreams, that we'd go into the next school year and things would fall into place. I had just signed Josh up for the football team and the school was considering allowing him back in mainstream classes. I wanted this to happen so badly that I wasn't being honest with myself about what was going on.

I arrived at camp just before dark. Josh hadn't packed his belongings and wasn't sure he wanted to leave after all. I sat in my car and sobbed. I was scared, exhausted and unsure how to take the next step. His rage towards me has gotten so bad that it goes from zero to red zone rage in a matter of moments. I wondered if I'd be able to get home safely. I wondered if I would be leaving without him. I felt simultaneously punched in the gut and like the rug had been pulled out from under me. All I could do was watch in horror as he slid quickly into the danger zone.

Somehow I pulled myself together and told Josh to get his stuff and load it in my car, but by then it was dark. His stuff was everywhere. We were using flashlights and the lights on our cellphones to find and throw his things into garbage bags and his footlocker. I cannot even imagine what we left behind. I waited in the car while he finished. I had no more fight in me. I was completely spent. I wasn't sure that I could make the drive home that night since the exhaustion was just too much. I wondered how risky it would be to try to stop for the night. In the end, I made the choice to drive straight through, dropping him at his dad's house shortly after 2:00 am. I drove home from there with the windows down, trying to keep myself from falling asleep at the wheel. Thankfully, I made it home and was able to get myself to the couch before I fell into a deep, restless sleep.

Chapter 18

• • • •

Josh's early return from camp filled me with mixed emotions. There was comfort in knowing that he was close by should something serious happen, but I was also scared that something even more serious would happen. I had called both his therapist and psychiatrist while on the way to pick up Josh at camp. I left them both messages, since it was often difficult to get an immediate appointment, and filled them in on his deteriorating mental health. I did not want Josh to go unchecked for very long. Luckily, they each could see him within a few days of his return.

The late July heat and humidity felt oppressive. Josh put the window down in my car as we drove to his therapist's office.

"It's just too hot for that today," I said putting the window back up with the button on my door.

"I can't stand being trapped in this car, I need the fresh air." His voice was tight. Josh had been unusually quiet for most of the drive, and I guessed that he was not in the mood to compromise.

I wanted to be considerate of what he was feeling, but the humidity was aggravating my asthma. A few minutes later, Josh put the window down again. Deciding that it wasn't worth a battle, I turned the air conditioning to full blast and left his window alone. Josh didn't balk at this move. We rode in silence the rest of the way.

He was still in a foul mood when he came out of the office 50 minutes later. "It was fine," was his only response when I asked how things went.

Even though he wasn't in a great mood, I was anxious to spend more time with him. "Feel like grabbing a cheeseburger and a milkshake?" I was trying to sound lighthearted and hopefully not too desperate.

"Just take me home," he replied. That word "home" struck me right in the heart. With Josh away at camp, it didn't feel so much like he had moved out, but hearing him say this made me realize that I was still mourning his move to his father's. In another time and space, I might have tried harder to persuade Josh to join me for a quick dinner, but I knew I'd be seeing him in two days for his psychiatrist appointment, and that would give me some extra time with him. I hoped by then he'd be in a better mood.

I joined Josh in his meeting with the psychiatrist. We assumed our "regular" seating arrangement in her office and I listened as he answered her questions.

"How are you feeling today?"

"Alright."

"Have you been thinking about harming yourself?"

"Not really."

"Not really?"

"No."

"What happened at camp?"

"My boss was a jerk, he wanted me fired the whole time."

"Hmmm."

"Really, from the very first day he was all over me, waiting for me to screw up!"

I stayed quiet. I really didn't know what had happened at the camp. When I spoke with the director or staff they had given me a very different story, but I realized the only thing that mattered was Josh's perspective on his experience.

"How have you been feeling since you stopped the Abilify?"

"Look, I know that I am not feeling as good as I did when I was taking those meds, but they made me feel like a zombie and I'm not going back on it."

I wanted to insert myself directly in the middle of the conversation. I had a dozen reasons why Josh should go back on the medication. While I wasn't a big fan of medication in general, keeping Josh safe and alive seemed to be a very good reason to pursue the option. It didn't have to be for the long-term, but long enough to stabilize his moods again. It was so hard to sit there and keep my mouth shut. Josh's decisions affected everyone. I finally turned to the doctor and asked, "Is there something else that Josh could try that doesn't have the same side affects?"

In fact, there was. She said, "There is drug that has been newly approved to be used by children under the age of 18 called Geodon. It is also an antipsychotic like Abilify, but there have been fewer complaints of weight gain or lethargy." The drug was normally prescribed for schizophrenia and bipolar disorders, but even though Josh was being treated for symptoms of depression and anxiety and had not been formally diagnosed with these or any other mental condition, the doctor felt that it would greatly help stabilize his moods and enhance his safety. "What do you think, Josh?" the doctor asked.

There was a long pause and finally, he said, "Yeah, I'm willing to give it a try."

I tried not to show my excitement, but after having seen the positive results Josh had had on the last medication, I felt hopeful that he'd be feeling better in no time. I believed that this episode was just a small setback and would soon be forgotten. I hoped and prayed that this were true.

Two days later, we were back in CPEP.

Josh and his girlfriend had decided, over the phone, that they were both going to end their lives at the same time. Later, Josh shared that they had both confessed their deepest, darkest pain to each other and felt that there was nothing left to live for in their lives. The plan was to overdose on pills, but before Josh ended the call, he encouraged her to share with her parents that she felt unsafe. Josh left the house with a pocket full of pills, deciding that he was going to go through with their plan anyway. Luckily, his stepmom noticed Josh leaving and went outside to see what was going on. After coaxing him back into the house, Josh broke down and admitted to his plan, scattering pills all over their kitchen.

I met Josh and his father at the emergency room. The routine through CPEP was the same as the past visits but this time, there were no beds in our local hospital and we'd have to wait for something to open up. We waited more than twenty-seven hours for a placement at an alternate hospital. An ambulance was necessary to transport him to the closest hospital with an open adolescent bed, which was an hour and a half away. I followed the ambulance.

I was back in the routine of treatment team meetings, family sessions, and visitation. I was grateful he was alive. It took three hours round trip just to spend a few minutes with him. Josh's father and I alternated visitation. This time, there was a look on Josh's face that I hadn't seen before: he seemed even more scared and unsure of himself. Each time I saw him, I felt waves of pure panic rise up through my whole being.

We started over again with a new treatment team in a different facility. This ward was smaller than the one Josh had stayed in previously. All of the patient rooms were right off the main common area, next to the nurse's station. The dining room doubled as the family conference room, reminding me more of being in a teacher's conference than a psychiatric treatment meeting. There was also a separate conference room outside of the ward that was used for a number of meetings between the treatment team and his father and me, where Josh was not included.

There were multicolored beanbag chairs in the room where I visited

Josh. It felt relaxed and informal. After a couple of days, Josh seemed to relax into the flow of the new hospital setting. "Did you know that we get to go outside every day?"

I had known, but I hadn't shared that with him because he was under assessment and I didn't want to get his hopes up. "That's great!" I said, and I meant it. Josh always loved being outside. He much preferred the cooler temperatures of fall and winter to the hot, humid summers but, given the fact that he was in the hospital now, he wasn't going to turn down the chance to go outside. The weather had been perfect, warm but not hot and it was gratifying to know that Josh was not fully missing out on the end of the summer.

Five days into his in-patient stay, I received a call asking if I could come in and discuss Josh's discharge criteria. The thought of a possible discharge put me into a panic. He hardly had the time to get settled in to the hospital, let alone time to stabilize. There were still occurrences of the rage, anxiety, and depression that had been prevalent since his initial breakdown.

I felt sick as I made my way to the hospital. The long drive only gave me time to imagine all of the possible and frightening scenarios that could unfold if Josh were released too soon. Josh's plan to die by suicide was not a joke. It was a factor that changed everything. How could I keep him safe? I wondered. I felt ill equipped to handle this. There had already been so many nights when Josh was at my house when I was doing round-the-clock suicide watch, setting my alarm every hour or so to get up and check on him. Even then, I knew it wasn't enough. But now, the reality of the situation was overwhelming. I didn't know how to keep my son alive.

My continued efforts to find support never resulted in any actual leads. I felt like I was an island, alone trying to support and protect this child whom I loved more than life itself. I recognized that this was beyond what I felt capable of handling, and I hoped that in my discussions with Josh's doctor, he'd be able to spell out some ways to address these concerns.

As I stood at the ward door waiting to be permitted to enter, I rang the buzzer for the second time. Unlike the first hospital, this door had no window, which made it impossible to tell if anyone was at the front desk. After a few minutes, I picked up the phone on the wall near the buzzer, and a nurse answered. There was a problem with the door, and no one was aware I was waiting. She asked me to have a seat in the hallway and let me know that the doctor would come out to meet me shortly. It was hard not to be frustrated. I was anxious, and the waiting only gave me more time to ruminate about how this meeting would play out.

Finally, Josh's social worker, Ned, met me in the hallway and I was escorted back to the doctor's office. I half-expected Josh to be standing there waiting for me as I walked through the common area, but Ned told me that the patients were out on the basketball court. "Maybe it is best that he doesn't know I'm here," I thought. A part of me felt disappointed because any chance I had to see his face made me happy.

"Your insurance provider is questioning the need for Josh's hospitalization," Dr. Kenney informed me.

"This is nothing new," I said. "It seems that within a few days of treatment, regardless of the need, the threat of discontinuation of service is suggested." I'd experienced this before.

Dr. Kenney seemed surprised. "I don't think I'll be able to convince them that Josh requires this level of care much longer."

I was confused. Josh was prepared to kill himself and now, six days later, he was safe to go home? "Do you feel that Josh is safe to go home?" I asked the doctor.

There was a long pause before Dr. Kenney told me that Josh had not threated to harm himself since he had been admitted and, even with Josh's other symptoms, he didn't feel that would be enough to convince the insurance company to continue to pay for treatment.

I stared at him in disbelief. "I'm not sure I know how to keep Josh safe," I admitted. "I've done round-the-clock watch and constantly check in with him when he's not home, but I feel under-equipped to support him"

Without missing a beat, Dr. Kenney said, "You are the parent and this is your job."

Of course it was my job. I wasn't debating that fact, but I was looking for support and guidance to help me through something that I'd never before experienced as a parent. This was life or death. "What do you suggest I do, then?"

"You can make him sleep in bed with you or sleep on your bedroom floor," he replied.

"What? Do you actually think that I can force Josh to sleep in my bedroom?" In any other situation, this conversation would be laughable. I was barely five foot tall. Josh stood taller than six feet and looked a bit like a linebacker, especially with the weight he'd gained from his medication. There would be no forcing Josh to do anything he didn't want to do; he'd already made that perfectly clear.

"We won't be keeping him hospitalized because you don't feel like you can take care of him."

That wasn't what I was saying at all. I left the meeting completely deflated. By the time we finished, it was dinner hour on the ward. I decided that I didn't want to interrupt Josh, especially because I could see him through the dining hall door and he looked peaceful, eating his dinner and chatting with some kids at his table. I'd be back tomorrow to visit. As I walked towards the door, though, I stopped and turned back towards the dining hall. I stood watching him for a few more minutes. It reminded me of how I used to stand in his room and watch him sleep; I had memorized the shape of his face and the way he breathed while in deep slumber. This time, I was memorizing his face just in case I never saw it again.

During our weekly family meeting, two days later, Dr. Kenney gave us an update on Josh's condition. Moods were stable. No threats of self-harm. There were a few incidents of defiance, but those were worked out without much fuss. "Josh, do you think you feel safe enough to go home?" Dr. Kenney questioned.

There was panic in his eyes "I - I don't know actually," Josh responded.

I could tell he meant it. Josh would not miss a chance to go home if he felt done with the program. I spoke up, "I don't think he is ready to go home, he's still not feeling safe and it's only been two days since he shared that he had thought of harming himself."

Dr. Kenney ignored my concerns, focusing back on Josh "You are going to have to go home at some point, what do you think about giving it a go?"

I was completely distraught. "He said he wasn't ready!"

Then Josh turned to me. I could see fear in his eyes as he said, "Mom, he's right. I'm going to have to go home sometime."

Four days later, he attempted suicide.

Chapter 19

• • • •

August 19, 2011

The suicide attempt is a major turning point; it's a game changer as far as I'm concerned. I can no longer trust that Josh is okay because he says so or because the doctors feel that "he has to go home at some point." Last night when the phone rang, even before I heard his father's voice, I knew that my deepest fears came to pass. Hearing the words that he had attempted suicide, how do I even describe it? It was at once surreal and almost too real for my brain to handle. I am grateful that Josh had survived, though he had a stomach full of pills and was on his way to the hospital when I received the call, so I didn't know what was yet to come.

Josh had saved his own life. After sneaking out into the woods near his dad's home, he consumed more than half a bottle of Tylenol, but then had second thoughts about what he had done. He called 9-1-1 and the police came to meet him. I was home in my bed asleep while this was happening. I know that there isn't anything I could have done to stop it even if he had been at my house, but I feel guilty. I am sick to my stomach as I think about what could have happened. What might have been different this morning had he not called the police? I am haunted by thoughts of how things might have ended differently.

I got out of bed, dressed, and met Josh at the emergency room. I remember the time on my dashboard clock reading 0:00 as I drove to the hospital. It felt significant, not in the fact that it was midnight, but that it made me think of a zero point. It was as though this was the point from which we would now be able to chart his progress, positive or negative, going forward.

When I got to the hospital, I found my way to Josh's room. He was angry and agitated. On a number of occasions throughout the night, security had to be called into his room to help calm him down. Eventually, he was moved out of the pediatric ER to a separate part of the emergency room where he wouldn't be disturbing the other patients. That was not the scenario I had expected, though as I sit here replaying it in my mind, I honestly don't know what I expected.

During the night, the doctor had Josh drink a charcoal mixture in hopes of counteracting the effects of the Tylenol on his liver. That was of the most concern, and we wouldn't know until morning if they were able to stop the poison from compromising his liver. If they had not, Josh would be in serious trouble. It was a waiting game. There was nothing else we could do but hold our breath and pray that the charcoal had been administered in time.

How did we get here? It seems like this continues to be the question on my mind. It's been 8 months since Josh's first visit to the ER and yet, I still am not able to wrap my head around what is happening. Twice I had to leave Josh to find a quiet restroom, just so to take a few moments to process. I wanted to scream, I wanted to be angry at God, at the situation, at the hospital that discharged him before he was ready. I realize that there is no one to blame. This somehow makes it even more unbearable. I stood in that tiny restroom, just steps away from where Josh was being treated, and cried.

✳ ✳ ✳

August 22, 2011

Thank God! Josh's liver was not affected by the overdose. I am so grateful. I haven't had much time to process this because once the results of the lab work came in, the ER began to process Josh for admission. Given the circumstances, we did not need to go through the CPEP route this time. Thank goodness, because the hospital we were at did not have a CPEP unit. Unfortunately, there were still no beds available locally, so we were sent back to the hospital an hour and a half away.

I'm still feeling conflicted by this because I truly feel that Dr. Kenney had discharged Josh too soon. Given the conversation I had with him just days before Josh's attempt, I assume that the hospital was under pressure by the insurance managed-care provider to move him out as quickly as possible. Still, I wonder if the fact that I shared my concerns about how challenging it was for me to know how best to care for Josh had any bearing on the decision. At this point, what is most important is that I will never, ever allow Josh to be discharged before he is ready. No matter what.

On my way home from visiting Josh today, I received a call from Child Protective Services (CPS). Apparently, a case has been open to investigate Josh's attempt. According to the caller, since this did not happen at my house, I was not under investigation. However, I was named in the investigation, and I should expect a call from the lead investigator in the next few days. When I asked how this incident would have been reported, she offered that Dr. Kenney had been the one who contacted them.

So the same doctor who pushed for Josh's early discharge, knowing that there was a threat of self-harm and suicide ideation, was the one who reported us to Child Protective Services. Had I not been so exhausted, this fact may have surprised me.

August 25, 2011

Josh's suicide attempt has made it clear that he is not ready, nor is it safe for him to be home. Yesterday, we had our first family meeting since his admission. Dr. Kenney recommended that Josh's medication be adjusted, because he suspects that the Geodon may have contributed to the speed of Josh's decline since he left the hospital last week. It's been recommended that he also discontinue Hydroxyzine, which he has been taking to help with sleep, and start Seroquel and Effexor at bedtime. It feels a bit like a game of alphabet soup with all these medications. At this point, what choice do we have? His life depends on getting this right. Unfortunately, it seems that the only way to find out if it's right is through trial and error. Knowing this does not make me any feel better.

It's being recommended that Josh be institutionalized in a state mental hospital. Both the doctor and social worker reported that they feel Josh's needs a longer-term care facility and services that cannot be offered in their in-patient program. The closest hospital is 70 miles away from here. There is a local hospital in our city, but it is in the process of being closed down due to funding cutbacks. The thought of Josh locked up in a state institution is twisting my stomach into knots.

The doctor had already prepared the referral prior to our meeting because the application reviews only occur once a week. We've been warned that even though it is his doctor's recommendation, the state facilities are at maximum capacity, and we needed to be prepared that his referral would be denied. Then what? What happens then? No one knew the answer. It is likely that once Josh stabilizes, he will be moved to a temporary facility while he waits for the decision. The only other option is to look for a private facility that would agree to accept Josh into their program.

Josh's father had already been searching for an alternative and has found a private facility in Maine that has a bed available. It's a big risk because if we choose to go that route, Josh's records will reflect that he was discharged from care against his doctor's recommendation. Doctor Kenney informed us that making this decision would take Josh completely out of the behavioral health system; this will mean that if he needs additional care or to be institutionalized down the road, we will have to start over at *the beginning of the process. How do I know what is truly best for my son? It is an agonizing decision.*

I just want to wrap my arms around him and hold him in my lap like when he was a little boy. I want to kiss all his boo-boos and make this all better. I can hardly breathe right now thinking about the pain he must be in, the painful thoughts that he has in his head and heart, painful enough to drive him to want to take his own life. I sit here and I feel like I'm drowning and cannot possibly get to the surface in time to fill my lungs with the air that I need to keep moving forward. And yet, I have no choice but to do just that. Breathe.

Chapter 20

• • • •

S ummer was quickly turning into autumn, though the burst of hot, humid air made it feel more like mid-July. It was the early setting sun and cooler nights that gave away the fact that the seasons were shifting. At this point, Josh had been in and out of four separate inpatient hospitalizations, plus had participated in numerous outpatient treatment programs and private therapy. All the while his mental health continued to deteriorate and his suicide attempt left me gasping for air.

My greatest concern was the fact that there had been no formal diagnosis. In the latest treatment team meeting, I asked why they were reluctant to diagnose. "Generally, we don't formally assess children under the age of eighteen, especially when symptoms are overlapping, like in Josh's case." Overlapping in that the symptoms could be linked to more than one possible diagnosis; his depressive moods could be indicative of clinical depression, but they could also indicate bipolar disorder. The reality was that there wasn't a simple blood test that could be ordered to definitively identify his illness. Yet, there was still a need to work within a context of the symptoms he was presenting so that treatment and medication could be prescribed and monitored. The lack of a clear diagnosis was frustrating, and it felt like a big piece of the puzzle was being overlooked.

During each hospitalization, there had been differing opinions and interpretations of Josh's experience, ranging from depression to bipolar and borderline personality disorder; one doctor even suggested that Josh's actions were all a ruse to get attention. Because of this, it was not unusual for the treatment and protocols to change as he went from one inpatient stay to another, the suspected diagnoses changing each time.

As far as I could tell, Josh's symptoms weren't changing dramatically, but they were definitely getting worse. The suicide attempt had served to demonstrate the seriousness of the situation. No one doubted that fact. There were also no conclusive answers for how to get Josh safely on the road to recovery.

I was myself at a loss. Throughout the crisis, I felt like I'd been thrown into the role of mental illness caregiver without any instructions, support or light at the end of the tunnel. Every chance I got, I was trying to do my own work to figure out what Josh needed and what I could do to impact the services and support he was receiving.

I wanted to figure out what was happening so that, at least in my mind, I could help Josh recover faster. I began to contemplate mental illness in all of its angles, faces and definitions. I felt as though having a better understanding of mental illness as it related to what was happening in my life could lead to better support for Josh. I also wondered if there was something else at play here, something that Josh wasn't sharing with me, that could help bring more clarity around the whole situation; but, as far as I could tell there was nothing.

I considered whether it was possible that the crisis my son was experiencing could be lumped into the bigger bucket called "mental illness," because the doctors didn't fully understand or know why he was acting and reacting to his emotions in a way that was harmful and unhealthy. I tried to look at the situation from every angle imaginable.

So many children and teenagers were in the same programs and hospitalizations with my son, each of them experiencing "mental illness" in some shape or form. I found it so difficult to wrap my head around why these children would want to harm or kill themselves. I posed a lot of questions to myself as I explored this question, though I cannot readily say that I came up with many answers. I struggle with this still.

* * *

While I was working to better understand Josh's crisis, I also tried to decide how much information I wanted to share with my employer. Even though nine months had passed since Josh's first trip to the emergency room, I had kept silent at work because I believed or wanted to believe that the end of the crisis was right around the corner, and didn't think a full disclosure was necessary.

Yet, there were other reasons why I wanted to keep this situation quiet. I didn't want to risk losing my job. My career was a big part of my identity, having played a prominent role in my life since I was fresh out of college. Being successful in business had always been very important to me, especially because I had struggled so much in school. I felt in some ways that my success would prove that I was smart enough, even if I couldn't demonstrate that in the traditional grading and test-taking fashion.

As a young business professional climbing the corporate ladder, I had everything going for me. Balancing a career and motherhood was always somewhat of a challenge, but it was something that I prided myself on being able to do in a way that I felt gave equally to both my family and my job. My career was always the means to an end. What I did for a living directly contributed to what I could do for my children and the life we were living. It directly contributed to how I measured myself as a good mother, equating what I could provide with how well I was able to care for my children.

When Josh's illness hit, I found myself in the middle of hell; the equilibrium that I had been able to maintain for so many years was completely thrown off by the fact that my child needed much more from me than the love and care I had been providing. Shifting the balance to provide more support was not in question, but maintaining some type of work and life balance proved difficult. It took a long time to find my way out of the labyrinth, both as I labored to navigate the mental health system maze but also as I fought to keep my head above water with my obligations to my job. Eventually, I found that I could plan around the timing of the many meetings, treatment team reviews, and medications check-ups and still meet my responsibilities.

Even before this crisis I had been assessing whether or not I was on the right career path. I had lost the passion for my position and the work I was doing. Facing the depth and uncertainty of Josh's circumstances, I decided that my career, even as it lay in shards on the ground, was going to have to take a back seat to the more pressing issues I was facing, knowing that at some point, I would have to address that crisis, as well.

Chapter 21

• • • •

The application for the state hospital did not get evaluated during the first review cycle. Josh's father and I became increasingly concerned that we were running out of time before the insurance company would force Josh's discharge.

Faced with the choice to either wait for a response from the state hospital or to pursue the private camp option, I contacted Josh's psychiatrist for guidance.

Over the phone, I brought the doctor up-to-date on Josh's progress and treatment since his suicide attempt and provided her with information about the private camp. While we were talking, I sent her the camp's website and contact information. "Give me a few days to review all of this information," she requested.

A few days later, I received her letter in the mail.

September 1, 2011

To whom it may concern:

Josh White has been under my psychiatric care since January 2011, in both my positions as inpatient attending psychiatrist at the hospital where Josh has been hospitalized multiple times, and as his outpatient provider.

Josh has tried all treatment opportunities and programs offered in our area and beyond. I have recommended a long-term residential setting for more intensive and comprehensive treatment for Josh, given his repeated hospitalizations for self-harm and suicidality. Since past behaviors are the greatest predicator of future behavior, Josh is at a very high risk of suicide.

The Therapeutic School for Teens offers the intensity and breadth of treatments I recommend for Josh at this time. At this time, Josh is disabled because of this medical condition. If he does not receive a more intensive treatment, one can expect his mental health to continue to deteriorate, and him to continue the patterns of suicide attempts.

Thank you,

Lisa Summer, M.D., Ph.D

Chapter 22

• • • •

September 11, 2011

I could not have imagined that things would get worse. I thought we'd hit the bottom. Having to make a decision about residential care and choosing between insurance-funded and privately-funded treatment was never something that I planned for. I have to keep reminding myself that at least I was not planning his funeral, though that was still a fear of mine. Since Josh's attempt, I keep replaying what could have happened. I don't want to think about it; I would rather focus on the fact that he is alive and getting treatment, but I cannot put it out of my mind.

I am not sure what I would do if I wasn't staying true to my yoga practice. The "40 days" program that I attended has helped me stay grounded, somewhat, in the midst of these turbulent days. Even though more often than not I lie on my yoga mat and cry through many of the classes, turning my phone off for that one hour a day has been a lifeline for me.

I've done a lot of crying lately. It seems that I've spent more than nine months crying. How can there still be tears left to shed? Every time I start to trust that things are going to turn around, I am jolted back to reality by yet another set of circumstances that remind me I am still deep in this crisis.

I had such great hopes for the private wellness camp in Maine. I figured that since the hospitalizations had done nothing to help get Josh on the road to recovery, it made sense to try something different. It was a risk to go to the camp. I knew this, but I felt that there was really no other choice. Given that there was a month-long waiting period before we'd know if there was a bed in the state institution, it seemed like the best decision.

Josh agreed to go along with the plan but, once there, it was a different story. As soon as he arrived, he wanted to leave. I don't blame him. I want him to come home, too. I want this whole damn thing to be over. The worst part of the process for new admissions was that there could be no direct communication between the parent and teen. I was not allowed to speak with him for 30 days. Thirty fucking days. Email was the only mode of communication. I sent him an email every day. He was allowed to write me letters, but that was the extent of the communication.

Early on, perhaps too early in hindsight, the therapist asked both his father and me to send an email letting him know that we were committed to his stay at the camp and we would not check him out early despite his vocal desire to leave. I knew through the social worker that Josh was begging and demanding the staff to tell us to come get him. It made me sick to think of him so far away and just wanting to come home. I sent the email as I was asked. It haunts me still because, in the end, it resulted in Josh running away from the camp.

I was standing in my parent's driveway when the phone call came in and I nearly collapsed. I was so panicked. Josh was in the middle of a remote part of Maine; it was getting close to evening. The police had been called. My mind went numb. What if they didn't find him before dark? How could they keep him safe? What in the hell had I done? The police, luckily, did find him, and he was transported to a local hospital.

This time, there was no possibility of me running to the hospital to sit with him. A staff member from the camp stayed with him throughout the night. I was kept abreast of the situation with a phone call every few hours. While Josh was stable, he was also threatening to take his own life if they made him go back to the camp. He even went into great details outlining his plan. I realized that the hopes I had held onto that this camp would be "the" place that would finally lead to his recovery had been dashed.

I am exhausted. I am beyond worried at this point. It felt like the camp was my last hope to keep him safe and alive. My mind cannot stop thinking about what will come next, what options there will be to get him the help that he needs. I cannot even contemplate this right now. I am beyond the ability to even believe that this is truly happening. Why can't I wake up from this terrible nightmare? Where is my old life? It wasn't perfect, but my son was healthy and we had a relationship that I miss so desperately. I am still having a tough time breathing through it all. I'm crying again. It's not even worth trying to stop at this point. I have never known pain to be so deep and hope to be so lost as it is at this moment.

Chapter 23

. . . .

D
r. DeMartin called first thing in the morning. It had been so long
since I'd slept through the night, I had already been up for hours
and was onto my second pot of coffee. It had been three days since
Josh had been admitted to the psychiatric ward. There had been no
other choice since he had threatened he would kill himself if I forced
him to return to camp. That was not a risk I was willing to take.

The doctor was returning my call from the day prior. My last call
with Josh had been eye opening; he had been vacillating between a calm
disposition and angry "I hate you's". It felt like we were riding a seesaw.
One minute he was up, and the next he was slamming into the ground.
In the middle of this exhausting conversation, Josh mentioned that he'd
told the emergency room doctor that he wanted to kill himself just so
that he wouldn't have to go back to the camp. It was no wonder I hadn't
slept the night before. I was sick with worry and in light of this new
information, I wasn't sure what to believe anymore.

"Mrs. White, my suggestion is that you take every threat seriously,"
the doctor counseled. "Remember, Josh is going through a very stressful
situation as well. He is angry and scared."

"I know." I could hardly reply through my sobs. "I cannot imagine
how he is feeling right now."

Dr. DeMartin suggested that we schedule a family meeting for the following day since she still wanted to complete her evaluation. I wasn't sure that I'd heard her correctly. "Wait, you are doing an evaluation?"

"Of course, why wouldn't I?"

"Because this will be the first formal evaluation he's had!" I wanted to shout into the phone. I didn't feel like going through the long answer to that question; it was easier to pretend that I was just verifying that I heard her correctly. My heart was pounding so hard I could feel it in my ears. I couldn't tell if I was anxious or excited. I felt like I had won the lottery and was hopeful that Josh was in the right place, even if he hadn't gotten there in a straight line. I couldn't wait to hear the results.

The assessment weighed on my head and heart. I glanced at the clock: it read 8:30 a.m. I knew it was going to be a long day. While I was initially excited by the thought of finally getting some answers to Josh's breakdown, the thought of not being physically present with him as he was informed of the doctor's findings made the situation feel even more unbearable.

The next morning, we met over conference call. It was nice to hear Josh's voice on the other end of the phone. He sounded calm and anxious about the results of the assessment as well. Since this was our first family meeting, the treatment team introduced themselves and shared a little about their role in Josh's care. It was similar to the teams I'd worked with in the past: there was an attending physician, a social worker, and a psychiatric nurse assigned as a team. They explained there would be other nurses and social workers on staff who would be involved as necessary to make sure Josh's needs were covered.

I felt impatient. I knew it was important to take the time to get to know the people who would be responsible for Josh's care, but I wanted to know the results of the assessment. Josh had been very quiet throughout the meeting so far, and I felt certain that he was as anxious for some answers, as well.

"Upon completing my assessment and reviewing Josh's history," the doctor began, "we are leaning towards a diagnosis of Type 2 bipolar." Dr. DeMartin shared that she felt Josh's behavior was out of control and that though she didn't feel he actually wanted to die, his impulsivity put him at risk for an accidental suicide, meaning that he could die from a self-harming situation not fully thought through. "We have come to the conclusion that Josh needs to be in a long-term care facility because it will provide a safe haven for him to work through these challenges."

I realized that I had been holding my breath. My mind was racing to comprehend what was being communicated. Type 2 bipolar? Accidental suicide? I was trying to take notes and still focus on the new information that was being relayed. "We believe that Josh would do well on a mood-stabilizing medication," the doctor continued. "I would like to have Josh begin Lithium this afternoon." I felt myself choke back sobs. I knew this was heavy-duty medication and, as I would soon learn, the side affects were risky.

Nurse Steller stepped in to give more information. "A blood draw will need to be ordered to start the process. This will give us a baseline on Josh's kidney and thyroid functions, as well as a starting point to measure the build-up of the medication in his blood stream." It would take some time to get Josh up to a therapeutic level. "A week to ten days is the typical timeframe. If there is any change to the kidneys or thyroid, we will need to discontinue the medication immediately," the nurse added.

I wanted to know how Josh was responding to this information, especially since he had been completely silent throughout this meeting. When the nurse was finished giving the lowdown on the next steps with the medication, she turned her attention towards Josh and asked if he had any questions. "Will it make me gain weight?" he asked.

I was relived that that was his biggest concern and his tone did not sound as though he was going to put up much of a fight. "No, Josh, but it will make you feel a bit sleepy for the first couple of days."

There was a long silence and finally an almost inaudible, "Okay."

Later that evening, I called the hospital to speak with Josh. The nurse seemed a bit hesitant and asked me to hold. Josh picked up the phone and he was screaming and yelling. I couldn't understand what he was saying. Finally, he calmed down enough for me to clearly hear, "I hate it here, Mom. I want to come home." What could I say? I hated that he was there, too. My heart was beyond broken for him, but I felt as though there was nothing more that could be done until we saw how he handled the new medication.

While I watched and waited to see how Josh would respond to this latest attempt to stabilize his moods and out-of-control behavior, I was still faced with the challenge of finding a long-term care facility that would accept his case. During our second family meeting just days later, the option of reopening the referral to the state hospital was mentioned. Josh's treatment team agreed to complete the appropriate paperwork. We all knew it was a long shot. Unfortunately, being that Josh was in a hospital in Maine and not in New York where he had initially been treated, there were some challenges. His treatment team did not have any specific information or direct route to process the out-of-state referral. I contacted Josh's clinician from his previous inpatient hospital, since he had been involved in the initial referral process. He agreed to help move the paperwork through the state referral procedure. We'd have to wait until the following week to find out if the application would be reviewed or postponed.

It was during this second family meeting that Dr. DeMartin announced that she was leaving for another assignment and that Josh's case would be transferred to a new doctor. I was in shock. These constant upheavals were bewildering. The doctor assured Josh that they'd meet again in the morning, but Josh remained silent; it was unsettling.

Josh's moods had been fluctuating in more rapid and unpredictable ways since he had arrived at the ward. The night nurse had been administering his Seroquel earlier in the evening in an attempt to quell some of his anxiety and the increased outrage that had been occurring at bedtime. Since it was recommended that nighttime phone calls be limited, I waited to call the night nurse to find out how things went after bedtime hours. On that particular night, I was anxious to find out what transpired, especially since Josh had been so quiet in the family meeting.

Nurse Steller was on duty when I called. She replayed the evening events that included Josh punching a wall and threatening to harm himself. Even with the earlier dose of medication, the nighttime seemed to make him much more anxious and unstable. "Josh does not seem to be willing to take responsibility for any of his actions, and we are concerned that he is putting the rest of the ward at risk." She said she would discuss an increase in the dosage of the Lithium with Dr. DeMartin the next day.

It was well after 4:00 am when I finally fell asleep. I couldn't stop worrying about the rapid decline in Josh's mental health. Many nights, just as I was falling asleep, I could swear I heard Josh calling my name but, that night, I heard nothing.

I received a voice mail message from Dr. DeMartin the next morning; somehow my phone ringer had been silenced and I slept through my alarm. The doctor indicated that her meeting with Josh had not gone well. He was very upset and was demanding to know when he could go home. No decisions had been made on his next placement, but it was explained to Josh that going home was not under consideration. Josh had grown increasingly more anxious as the meeting continued, leading the doctor to put the nursing staff on notice to watch for signs of self-harm or threats to others.

By mid-afternoon, Josh's anxiety level had escalated so high the doctor was recommending adding a secondary stabilizer to the Lithium. I received a call from the on staff nurse asking for my permission. As we spoke, I did an Internet search for the drug Depakote, and found it was an antiseizure drug that worked as a stabilizer and would start to work faster than Lithium. The two combined were used in cases where the patient wasn't responding fast enough to the Lithium alone. "I approve," I told her. What else could I say? At that point, I couldn't even feel hopeful that the combination would do the trick.

✳ ✳ ✳

The next several days went by in a blur; I glanced at the calendar and felt confused when I realize that it was the end of September. Time had no meaning. Days muddled into nights; family meetings, medication updates and working to secure a placement for Josh took up all my time. Things continued to go from bad to worse. The Lithium dosages were raised and then raised again. The Depakote increases followed suit.

Dr. Luntz had differing diagnoses than his predecessor. While he agreed with Dr. DeMartin's assessment of Type 2 bipolar, he felt that Josh also exhibited symptoms that indicated borderline personality disorder and disrupted behavior disorder, as well. Just a few weeks earlier, we had no formal assessment or diagnosis to work with, and now we had three. "Josh has regression issues and a lot of deep anger that he has not dealt with," Dr. Luntz advised. "This coupled with the inability to clearly think through his actions and have insight into those actions is a very dangerous combination."

The transition between doctors had been seamless. I wasn't sure that Josh or I could handle starting this process over again. Even with a differing opinion on the diagnosis, Dr. Luntz explained that the treatment protocol would still be effective. The Lithium levels were finally beginning to rise, but not to the level that made a notable difference in Josh's behavior.

"The major concern is the level of mood irritability and thought processes that Josh is exhibiting," he explained in our next family meeting. " The chronic issues of self-harm, thoughts of suicide and the prior suicide attempt are major areas of concern." The doctor agreed that Josh was in need of long-term care. The serious nature of Josh's current state was not lost on anyone. I felt powerless and heartbroken that I was not able to do more to make him feel better. Wasn't that my job? Yet there was nothing I could do.

The state hospital application had still not been reviewed. Making the choice to take Josh out of the system and attempt the private camp had created complications and delays, but that was expected. He was nowhere near ready to make a move. We had time.

Two days later, Dr. Luntz called to inform me that they were preparing Josh's discharge paperwork.

"Discharge?" I stammered. "What do you mean discharge? He isn't ready to leave the hospital. His medication levels have not even stabilized!" I realized then that I was screaming into the phone. I kept thinking that this cannot be happening. This cannot happen. I regained some composure. "Someone has made a terrible mistake. Josh is nowhere near ready to be discharged."

The phone line was silent. For a moment, I thought that the call had dropped. "Hello?" I said.

"Yes, I'm here," Dr. Luntz replied.

"What the hell is going on?"

Again silence. Finally the doctor began to speak. "The managed care provider for your insurance company has notified us that they will not pay for Josh's services after tomorrow."

In the midst of Josh's escalating crisis, I had forgotten about issues I had faced early on with the managed-care provider. This time, however, Dr. Luntz had the name and phone number for a contact and suggested that I call directly.

* * *

Tears streamed down my face as I waited for my call to connect. My hands were shaking. I could not believe this was happening.

"Hello, this is Jessica," a voice said.

As soon as she answered the phone, I began to unload nine months of fear, angst and frustration. "Do you know how hard I have been working to keep this child alive and now you want to cut his benefits because you don't think he needs treatment? What if this were your child? How would you feel if someone were making a decision about care based solely on money and not on the health needs of your child? We have been through too much and come too far to allow this to happen!" I was certain much of what I said was unintelligible. I did my best through my choking sobs to let her know that there was no way in hell Josh would be discharged before he was stable, and if they did and something happened, it would be on their heads.

Jessica waited patiently for me to finish. "I've been following Josh's case since his second admission" she offered.

"What?" I was shocked. "Why the hell didn't I have your information before now?"

Jessica explained that there was no decision on Josh's discharge, but due to the number of days he'd been hospitalized, the hospital had been informed that his case was under review. It was standard operating procedure. However, if it was determined that further treatment was not necessary, they would cease paying for Josh's care. The managed-care provider's doctor, with input from Josh's attending doctor, had the final say as to whether or not further treatment would be necessary.

I couldn't sit back and wait, so I launched my own personal campaign to keep my son in the hospital; I engaged the human resources organization that managed the relationship between my company and managed care provider. I wrote letters to the hospital's attending physician, the treatment team, the vice president of psychiatric care and the vice president of client services, and included a whole package documenting my son's history and treatment up to that point. I also included the letter from my son's previous attending psychiatrist that had been written just before this particular hospitalization.

If they were going to discharge my son before he was ready to safely go home, I was going to put them all on notice that their discharge decision went against all of the medical information and recommendations that had been provided on his progress to date.

I was successful in securing additional time to continue his services, but only under the condition that we found a suitable residential facility that was within the insurance provider's network. The acute support that the inpatient program provided did not meet Josh's needs. Jessica provided a list of facilities that had open beds, and it was my job to decide which one was best for him. Looking at the list of facilities, I wondered, "How the hell do I choose the best place, and what happens if I make the wrong decision?" I guessed I would be finding out.

Josh was furious; he wanted to come home, and he saw the potential discharge as his chance to get there. I felt like I was stuck in the middle of a nightmare between wanting desperately for him to come home and for life to return to normal and not wanting to put him in a situation where he'd have an opportunity to kill himself. My heart still breaks when I think of all the times I had to make decisions that I felt would keep him safe, even as he blasted me and accused me of making those choices simply because I did not want him to come home. If I had to do it again, I would still make the decision that I thought would help to keep him alive.

Within days, I had found a facility that met the criteria of the managed-care provider, and it turned out that my choices were even more limited since only one of the options had available beds - the only challenge was it was 500 miles away.

Chapter 24

• • • •

O ctober 2011

The second day of October. This year has been simultaneously the longest and shortest of my life. I feel that I am trapped in a strange vortex of time. Was it just a year ago that things started to shift for Josh? Was it only twelve months ago that I was in a meeting with his school counselor, trying to counteract his inevitable slide? I could not have imagined how my life would play out over this past year. I don't think that I could have even made this up if I tried.

Yet, here I am. I've just completed the paperwork for Josh to be admitted into a 45-day assessment at a residential facility more than five hours from here. I've never seen it in person, though the website looks lovely. I am having trouble keeping my mind from creating horror stories of how it will be different than what it appears. What if he gets there and it's dirty or dangerous? What the hell have I done?

My last conversation with Josh was brutal. He is so angry with me for making this decision. He says that he will never forgive me for "locking him up." The decision to move him to residential care wasn't solely made by me, but there's no rationalizing this with him. I didn't even try.

Josh will move in two days. The paperwork is done and the schedule is set with both the hospital and the residential facility. After lengthy discussions about the safest way to transport Josh over the 8-hour trip,

I agreed with the treatment team's recommendation to move Josh by ambulance. The hospital placed the request with the ambulance company and received confirmation that Josh's transport was scheduled.

Then last night I received a call from the ambulance company explaining that they would require a payment of 50% of the cost of transport before they would commit to the trip. From what I was able to gather, this ambulance company had been bilked by the insurance company before and did not trust that they would receive payment. My insurance coverage included medically necessary transport in full, but when the ambulance company called for a pre-approval, the insurance company would not provide one. I did not have the $3500 available to pay for the services, so the ambulance company refused to schedule the trip.

It's all too much. This whole month has felt like one step forward and two steps backward. Nothing is going smoothly, and everything is hanging in the balance. I feel like I have been sent into battle over and over again. I am not complaining; Josh's life and his health are worth all of it and more. There's a part of me, though, that wishes that it could just be a little easier.

I did the only thing that I could think of doing at the time; I reached out to my company's human resources organization and found the person responsible for managing the relationship with the insurance company. This time, I wasn't dealing with the managed-care provider but instead directly with the insurance company, so this meant I needed to get a hold of a whole different group of people. It took quite a few calls and emails back and forth and, finally, I was given the word that the insurance company had approved the transport. Thankfully, my contact at the ambulance company had the same information when I called the next morning to confirm that Josh's transport had been finalized.

I'm crossing my fingers that there are no further issues with this move. I'm packed and ready to make the five-hour drive to meet the ambulance when it arrives at the new facility. I haven't seen Josh for over a month. I hope that I can hold myself together and get him settled in without any issue. My nervous system is already in overdrive as I think about tomorrow.

Chapter 25

• • • •

October 21, 2011

O*ctober 21, 2011*
It is not quite mid-way through Josh's forty-five day psychiatric assessment. To say that things have gone smoothly would not be entirely accurate. It's been a rough start to this chapter of his treatment. In the days leading up to his move, Josh had become irate and was refusing to be transferred. His clinician, Misty, called to get my permission to add a tranquilizer to his daily regimen to help calm him down and keep him safe.

I cannot imagine how scared and powerless Josh must have been feeling. A few times I actually considered changing my mind and bringing him home. I could hear the stress and the fear in his voice. I was constantly questioning myself about whether this was the right decision but, in the end, I knew it was the only decision that could be made.

On the morning of his relocation, Josh fought with his doctor and hospital staff as they tried to ready him for the move. The tranquilizer they'd administered wasn't doing enough to calm him down, so Nurse Steller called to get permission for something stronger to assist them in getting him into the ambulance.

I was praying that Josh would calm down enough to safely get into the ambulance. I didn't want to drug him. None of this was happening the way I had hoped. I asked the nurse if there was anything else they could do, but it had become a safety issue not just for Josh but for the staff, as well. Reluctantly, I agreed to the medication.

I cannot stop thinking about what he must be going through. I would have been so scared and anxious not knowing what was going to happen next. More than anything, all Josh wanted to do was come home. He had made that clear. He begged and pleaded. My heart broke more and more each time. I'm constantly wondering if I am I doing what is best for him. I have no idea. I'm just trying to keep him safe and alive.

Shortly after the additional medication was administered, the hospital called to let me know that Josh was in the ambulance and they were leaving for Pennsylvania. Pete and I got on the road so that I could meet the ambulance transport when it arrived from the Maine hospital. The drive was only five hours and it was expected that the ambulance would take between 8- 10 hours, but I wanted us to get there early to take care of all of the necessary paperwork and preparation ahead of time.

The medication was still in effect when Josh arrived at the facility. I hadn't seen him in more than 30 days. He looked worn out and disheveled. I wanted to just hold him in my arms and rock him and tell him that everything was going to be all right. When Josh saw me, he gave me a big hug. Even knowing that it was partially because of the drugs, I was grateful to wrap my arms around him. I could feel my heart pounding in my chest and I wondered, "How much more pain and sadness can I actually endure before I physically become ill myself?"

There wasn't much time to process that thought further because as the medication wore off, his anger returned and getting him settled in became a challenge. It's no wonder he is so angry with me; how could he not be? There I was, the one checking him into this facility; I was an easy target for his blame. Josh began demanding that I leave. He didn't want to see my face because it made him remember that he was in this terrible place and that I put him in this awful situation.

The staff was very compassionate and they were able to help Josh calm down, calm enough for him to eat a bit of the dinner I'd brought for him and for us to get the final paperwork signed. I was grateful that I was able to stay until he was going to bed.

We stayed the night in a hotel nearby and had a list of items that he would need to make his stay more comfortable. I was exhausted, but it made my heart happy to be making a late-night shopping trip to pick up clothes, a clock radio, and headphones for his iPod. Of course, I threw in a few extra things like flannel sleeping pants and a zip-up hoodie sweatshirt that I knew he would like. I didn't know what else I could do, but I wanted him to know that I really loved him. Maybe one day he would look at the sleeping pants and sweatshirt and know that I had done my best even in the worst of situations.

Over the first twenty days of the assessment, things were going fairly well. He had stabilized on his medication and was attending school on campus. During one of my visits, which were roughly every other week (his father's visits were opposite ours), he even walked with Pete and I up into one of the apple orchards on the property, showing us the views and the trails that he was able to hike. I was happy that he was able to connect with the outdoors here. He had been hospitalized for so long that he didn't have much of an option to get outside. It warmed my heart to see life in his eyes again as he shared this special part of his world with me.

There were still many ups and downs; his volatile mood swings and resistance to treatment and programs were concerning for the treatment team, as they were assessing whether or not he would be safe to come home. Even so, he had progressed enough to begin taking him off campus for short periods of time.

These off-campus visits usually revolved around a good steak dinner for him and a quick stop at his favorite stores in the mall. He has even been allowed to spend the night at my hotel on more than one occasion. I don't mind making the five-hour drive one way to be there in time to pick him up on Friday night; in fact, I am happy to do it. I want to do it. I miss him terribly, and often can't hold back my tears when I drop him back off at the facility at the end of our visitation.

While the formal review is still a few weeks away, the treatment team prepped me that their assessment was heavily focused on the need for further residential care. Maybe things will improve significantly between now and then. Maybe he will be stable enough to finally come home. As much as I want this with all my heart, I also want him to be safe, and his safety is foremost in my mind right now. I'm still afraid that if I make the wrong decision, he will end his life. I cannot bear the thought of this, but it is my reality.

* * *

October 31, 2011

More than ten months have passed, and I've still been unable to find any kind of true support, peer or otherwise. Seems mind-boggling to me, as I put it on paper. This means that for more than three quarters of this year I've flailed, trying to find my own path forward out of the darkness. While there have been times I thought I saw light at the end of the tunnel, the moments have been brief and almost as if a mirage.

Even when I started to share the story with others, it was met with silence. There were many whispers of, "How are you?" and lots of "thinking of you" or "praying for you," but the support has not been there. I'm so blessed to have my husband and a couple of close friends who have held my hand, my head and my heart through these dark days, but I cannot help but think that if I was dealing with a more "socially acceptable" disease, the outpouring of support would have been mind blowing.

Last night in yoga class, as I laid in Savasana pose, I had this sudden epiphany of how there is a huge rally of support when families experience a physical health crisis. People cook for you, clean for you, check in on you. There are fundraisers, walks, corporate sponsorship and awareness campaigns. While I do not bemoan this, I am being honest when I say that there is none of this community support and fanfare for a mental illness crisis. While I am truly grateful for those who have reached out to lend a hand, there has been very little of this for me.

As I was lying there at the end of my yoga class thinking about this, I kept wondering about ways that this situation could change. I wonder what could change to bring greater awareness to these circumstances. I am starting to believe that the reason why it's so hard to find support is in part because of the misconceptions and even the popular culture that paints mental illness in such a negative light. I wish that I knew how to help people understand that mental illness is not contagious, that there is no need for blame or to figure out why someone is experiencing such a crisis. Mental illness is just as life-affecting as any physical disease or illness, and yet that bridge of understanding seems too hard for some people to cross.

I think of all times I have sat up all night long worrying about whether Josh would take his own life, knowing that I have no control over the outcome of his crisis and praying – no, pleading - to God for his support and protection. There's no doubt in my mind that we are dealing with a life-threatening illness, no matter what name the illness is called. It is obvious to me that Josh's illness is equally scary and potentially life-ending as any other terminal disease. After five psychiatric hospitalizations, each time not knowing what the next steps would be or whether there would ever be a light at the end of the tunnel, I am constantly wondering if I will end up burying this child no matter what my best efforts might be to keep him healthy and out of harm's way.

I've found that most people don't want to talk about mental illness. In fact, even people who are going through a mental health crisis don't want to talk about it. I cannot even count the number of people who have been visibly uncomfortable when I've shared the story of what I've been going through with Josh. Worse has been the reaction from people when I shared about my son's suicide attempt. The silence and judgment that all too often follows has been heartbreaking.

It is so interesting as I sit and think about this; I wonder why it has to be this way. It makes it so much harder on me, feeling unsupported and worse, feeling judged instead of held and accepted. If someone had told me twelve months ago that my son was going to have a total breakdown, move from my house, share his belief that I was to blame, harm himself through drug and alcohol use and cutting, attempt suicide, have five hospitalizations, and would be living in a private residential treatment center, I would have thought **they** were crazy. I would not have believed it.

Maybe if the situation was reversed and I was hearing this story from someone else's perspective, it would have made me uncomfortable, as well. Perhaps I would have judged them, deciding that it must be their poor parenting that "caused" the situation, or their lack of "control" over their children. It's possible that I would have instead seen the face of my son in their story. It's just so hard to tell.

Chapter 26

• • • •

The assessment report was delivered to me on a warm, late-fall afternoon, in a room full of my son's treatment team, teachers, house guardians, and even some staff I had never met. Due to an illness, Josh's father joined the meeting over the phone. It was daunting, waiting for Josh to arrive to hear his "verdict." I had already had conversations with the treatment team and knew that, more than likely, home was not the option that they would be recommending.

As I sat there, my heart was breaking. I wanted to scream out to the entire room, "I just want my son to come home!" but I knew that wouldn't help the situation. The reality was that Josh could go home at any time; no one was forcing the decision to continue to seek treatment. The choice was a constant weighing of what was best for him based on the recommendations from the medical staff and whether it appeared he was safe to leave treatment.

Maybe screaming would have made me feel better. Over the course of this crisis, I have been regularly practicing car screaming. I'm sure that the other drivers on the road, if they caught a glimpse of me while engaged in this activity, would have thought I was unwell myself, but the huge release of emotions that came from a few good blood-curdling screams was undeniable and truly helped me process some of my deepest pain and sorrow through the challenges of these past months.

I was deep in my thoughts and still considering the option to scream out loud when Josh entered the room. He walked in with a playful strut that surprised me. His mood seemed nonchalant and carefree. I wondered if he knew something that I did not. I had not prepared myself for the possibility that I might be leaving the campus on this very afternoon with Josh in the car, headed home and onto his next chapter. I felt a moment of panic, wondering if he would truly be safe and ready to make that transition.

One by one, the members of his treatment team took turns sharing their assessments of Josh's situation and progress. "His school work has been improving, and he's been advanced to the next classroom," one of his teachers reported.

"Josh has been participating in group therapy sessions and respects his housemates when it's their turn to share," said his group leader. As each staff member reported out, I watched Josh's reaction out of the corner of my eye. He was handling the information as I had expected: he was angry and getting angrier. Even though much of the assessment shined light on the good work he'd been performing, he knew what was coming.

When it came to the doctor's evaluation, things were not as positive. "Josh continues to have impulsive behaviors, has demonstrated unhealthy choices, and continues to have episodes of suicidal ideation." I realized I was holding my breath. As I exhaled, the doctor continued, "We have not seen enough progress in these areas to believe that Josh would be safe outside of a residential care facility at this time." As the doctor made this recommendation for continued residential placement, Josh stood up and tossed aside his chair. My heart broke as I witnessed his anger and disappointment.

"Josh, why don't you sit back down so we can finish this meeting," his clinician suggested. Josh stood there, not saying a word, staring at the room full of what he must have believed were his adversaries. My heart skipped a beat, nervous about what was going to happen next. No one said a word as we watched and wondered about his next move.

Suddenly, he turned and ran out the door. The clinician excused himself to follow after him. While the facility was located in a somewhat remote area, no one was taking any chances that he'd try to head off the property. One of Josh's house guardians stood a moment later, deciding to offer assistance if necessary to ensure Josh was safe. We all sat in silence for several moments before a voice over the conference phone began to speak.

I had forgotten that Jessica from the managed care provider had been invited to attend this meeting. I had hoped she would be an advocate for the funding of Josh's continued care, should the recommendation call for additional residential treatment. "We will not be authorizing a continuation of services for Josh," Jessica said. Everyone in the room remained silent. Jessica continued, "In fact, at this time, we will not be extending any further benefits."

Jessica went on to explain that in order to continue to ensure my son received the recommended treatment and support, I had to find a placement in our home state so that Medicaid could supplement payment where the insurance company left off.

I argued that during his time at this residential facility, he had shown the most progress since the start of the crisis. "I cannot imagine that it is wise to move him now," I protested. However, even the treatment team agreed that a placement closer to home would be ideal, especially as weekend home visits would be a necessary step in his ultimate transition home.

Josh's clinician reentered the room. His face looked calm and even before he spoke, I knew that Josh was all right. "He didn't go far, in fact I found him just a few steps outside the door." He turned to me and said, "The house guardian walked him back to his room, but Josh wants you to stop by before you leave." I was relieved and grateful for the invitation, even though I would not have left without seeing him anyway.

I turned my attention back to Jessica on the conference phone. "I imagine it's going to take some time to figure out our next steps and secure a new facility for Josh. Will the insurance company agree to cover his care until we can move him?"

There was a long pause on the line before she said, "I will see what I can do." The challenge would be to find a placement for him before the insurance company decided to stop paying for his care. Even if they did, I knew I had no choice but to figure out a way to make sure that he received the services necessary until he was ready to come home.

✳ ✳ ✳

The following day, I engaged my county's Office of Mental Health to obtain placement approval and Medicaid authorization for Josh to move to a facility close to our home. I had to call several times before I was finally able to leave a message. I had no idea where to start or whom to talk with, but I felt an incredible sense of urgency to get the processing moving forward.

Keith Fine returned my call a few hours later. I'm not sure what I was expecting but, given how much pushing and fighting for Josh's care I'd been faced with previously, I was expecting a difficult process. I was pleasantly surprised with the level of compassion Keith showed about the situation and how helpful he was in outlining what would be required to get Josh into a county facility with Medicaid approval. "The process usually takes between forty-five to sixty days to secure placement," Keith shared as we neared the end of our call.

"I don't have forty-five to sixty days." I could feel the panic rising inside me. My heart was beating so hard I could hardly hear Keith's response.

"The biggest issue right now is that the board that approves the incoming residential placements only met once per month, and you've already missed the deadline for the next approval meeting."

That meant that Josh's application would not even go in front of the board for review for another five weeks. "Is there anything we can do to get an exception?"

Keith asked me to hold while he checked into a few things. As I waited, I found myself staring out my window; dusk was already blurring the view of the front yard, even though it was barely 5:00 p.m. The weather had turned colder since Halloween, and it was expected that we'd have measurable snowfall any day. "I need to get him closer to home before the snow falls, otherwise the drive through the mountain pass will be treacherous," I said, thinking out loud. I'd already had a few nerve-racking trips through rain and fog during recent visitation weekends.

Keith's return to the phone line startled me back to the present moment. "I've checked with the secretary, and the board does not have a full slate of applications for this coming meeting."

I let out an audible sigh of relief. "Okay, what do I need to do?" The challenge to overcome was that the meeting was happening in four days, but the application, doctor's input, and record gathering would take a significant amount of work.

I was up for the challenge. What choice did I have? Not only was I concerned about Josh's benefits being cut off, but also I really wanted Josh to be closer to home, especially with his birthday and Christmas not too far in the distance.

"Great! If you can quickly pull the package together, I will personally walk the application into the board meeting next Tuesday," Keith Fine said.

It was Friday night, and I knew I could only complete part of the application package over the weekend. I hoped that on Monday I'd be able to get a hold of Josh's records and other input from his doctors in time to meet the cutoff. It was a gamble, but there was nothing to lose by taking the chance.

The application and all corresponding paperwork was scanned and emailed to Keith Fine the morning of the review. Josh's residential facility, surprisingly, was the hold-up for the last pieces of necessary information. Regardless, Keith stayed true to his word and hand delivered the application for the board to consider. The clock seemed to move in slow motion through the late morning and into the afternoon. "Generally, the meeting is over before 4:00 pm, and you'll have your answer today," Keith shared when I called to confirm the receipt of the application. That particular day, it felt as though time was standing still.

The ringing phone startled me and I jumped to my feet while I answered. "Hello?"

"Congratulations, Josh's placement has been approved. In the next few days you'll be contacted by the admissions director of several local facilities and you can set up a tour."

I thanked Keith and hung up the phone as I collapsed into my chair. Deep sobs pulsated through my body. The anxiety and exhaustion combined with pure adrenalin had caught up with me.

It took a few more days than expected, but I eventually got in touch with one of the facility directors and scheduled a tour. The campus was less than 20 minutes from my house and sat on an 80-acre, predominately wooded estate, which was once bucolic farmland. The residents were lodged in English-style cottages, built originally in the early twentieth century when it had been used as an orphanage.

It was a beautiful late-autumn day. The sun was surprisingly bright, and I enjoyed the warmth on my face as I toured the facility. There were five cottages in all. The boys and girls had separate living quarters, and there were separate cottages for those in court-ordered treatment. The cottage where Josh would reside was midway across campus from the administration building.

While I waited to be buzzed into the house, I noticed a group of boys walking past. They were laughing and passing a basketball between them, heading, I was told, for some open time on the courts adjacent to the school building. In my mind, I pictured Josh there laughing and joking with the other boys. Those thoughts helped me feel just a little more peaceful about this decision.

Inside the cottage, I saw the dining room, recreation room and gaming room on the first floor, and then went upstairs to see the bedrooms and bathrooms. The upstairs was going through a bit of a remodel, and one of the residential counselors was getting ready to paint the hallway bright blue in preparation for an under-the-sea themed mural that she would be painting. "The boys got to vote on what theme they wanted," she shared, excited about the prospect of covering up the beige-colored walls. "It should really breathe some life into this place!"

Walking back to my car after the tour, I felt like things were finally falling into place. I really liked the facility and felt grateful that Josh would be so much closer to home. The administration office would need to review all of the paperwork and get the appropriate authorization from the Office of Mental Health, but they felt confident that by the middle of the next week we could begin planning for Josh's move.

A few days later, I received the news that Josh's admission application was accepted and we could begin making arrangements to move Josh. I hung up the phone after setting a date for his arrival and smiled, thinking, "Success! Finally in the middle of this nightmare, there's some positive news."

Moments later, my phone rang again. It was Jessica from my managed-care provider. "I figured you heard already, but just in case I wanted to make sure you know that Josh's care was terminated 3 days ago." I could feel the blood drain from my face. I was seven days from moving him and having Medicaid pick up the cost, and this provider had dropped my son and didn't bother to inform me until three days later.

The decision for the dropped coverage was made by the managed-care provider's doctor, who, in a conversation with the residential facility's doctor, was told that Josh's condition had not gotten worse and therefore it was determined that he no longer required residential care, even though I was moving him to another residential facility under the recommendation of the attending doctor and treatment team.

Again, I launched a full court campaign engaging my HR organization, the residential facility, and the Office of Mental Health. I was able to successfully get the managed-care provider to change their coverage decision, and they agreed to provide funding through the move date. I cannot imagine how things might have turned out for us had I not been able to engage the proper resources and fight for the support Josh required.

In the middle of one of the worst experiences of my life - caring for my ill child - I had to somehow find the strength to stand up and fight for his care over and over again.

Chapter 27

• • • •

January 2012

It was been one long roller coaster ride since Josh moved to his latest residential facility. In some ways there have been really positive things that have occurred; for instance, one benefit of Josh's move is that I was finally aligned with a family advocate. I was pleasantly surprised to learn, on the day Josh was admitted, that the facility had a program where they assigned a volunteer advocate to each new family. While we've only worked together for a month or so, having someone in my court feels good. It was a long time coming; I had spent quite a bit of time trying to find peer support on my own, but to no avail. It has been nice to have this level of connection.

Josh has settled in fairly well all things considered, but being so close to home makes it very challenging for him. I look forward to his weekend home visitations, even if he chooses not to spend them with me. We've had some nice times together, including celebrating his birthday and Christmas, almost like the old days.

It's been hard to gauge his progress, though. His treatment team reviews are good; his school reviews are good, too. In fact, he submitted one of the essays that he wrote in class for publication with the help of his English teacher. We won't know for a couple months if his piece will be accepted, but he's a great writer and I am almost certain we'll be seeing it in print. The family meetings and one-on-one therapy sessions, however, have gotten much harder to participate in. While Josh seems to have stabilized on so many levels, his anger is still hard to predict. Even within a therapy session, we can start out speaking about progress and next steps and then suddenly he is lashing out.

I'm truly exhausted. I continue to try everything I can to show him that he is loved and that I want nothing more than for him to come home. I want nothing more for him than to come home safely. I cannot imagine starting this process over if he is discharged and is not truly ready to integrate back into his former life. As I sit here right now, I have to admit that I am not sure I will survive another year of this intensity.

Perhaps I will always feel this way: always wondering if Josh is okay, watching for signs that he may be shifting into an unhealthy place. I suppose this is the road to recovery. I know it's not a straight path, and I know that there may always be a place of worry and watchfulness within me. This doesn't mean that I think he cannot continue his recovery; on the contrary, I believe that he can and will. I guess time will tell on this one. I am doing everything I can to surrender and trust that he will be okay.

If he continues to progress, my guess is that he will be home by the summer. While there has been some talk of a halfway transitional housing program before he finally goes home, my guess is that he won't need it. I am hoping that he can finish out his school year. What an accomplishment for him already, with everything he's been through, to be on track to complete his junior year of high school. I am really so proud of the work he is doing.

I think about what he'd say if he were reading this, wondering if all I care about is school. I know that it's not high on his list of things he cares about right now, but I cannot help but feel that completing high school will give him a sense of accomplishment. I have no doubt he will find his way, one way or the other. I guess I just feel like this is such a big mountain and if he can climb it now, it will be much easier than climbing it later.

What I am not writing about because it feels too hard right now is how our relationship continues to dissolve. It's hard to imagine that there is *anything left to fall apart, but there is quite a bit of anger and blame that is still being spewed my way. And while I've been down this road now for over a year, it doesn't hurt my heart any less. In fact, in some ways I think that it hurts my heart more now. I wish I knew why it feels this way, but it truly does.*

I guess what I really need to focus on is how grateful I am that, throughout these past months, my son's condition has shown significant improvement and, even more than that, I am grateful that he is still alive. Just the other day, I realized something really important in this whole journey: I would trade my relationship with him fully and completely in exchange for knowing that he is still alive and walking this earth. To me, that is much more important than anything. I just don't know what I would have done - or would do, for that matter - if he were successful in taking his own life. I hope that I never find out.

Chapter 28

. . . .

One of the benefits of having Josh so close to home was having the opportunity to take him to his appointments. When he was out of state, if he required dental or eye care, someone from the facility would transport him, and this always made me sad. Being present with him - even during routine check-ups - was something that I wanted to be a part of and that I valued.

It was an early March day, warm for late winter, and I decided to make a day of Josh's eye doctor appointment. I picked him up right after dismissal from school and we headed to a late lunch at one of our favorite burger joints. "My English teacher told me that my essay is going to be published!" he shared in between huge bites of his fried egg-topped hamburger. Josh was beaming. Things felt good and calm between us.

Earlier in the week, we'd had a chance to talk about some of the areas where he felt I'd let him down. It was a challenging conversation, but one that felt raw and honest and unlike many of the therapy sessions we'd attended together over the past months. There was no screaming and yelling on Josh's part. "I know that you had to travel for work when I was younger, but it made me feel like you were abandoning me," he had shared when I asked him to tell me about the times when I had let him down. "I know now that it was what you needed to do for your job, but back then I missed you, you know?"

Yes, I did know. "I missed you too, Josh, I missed you every single time that I had to travel." I couldn't hold back my tears. My heart broke for us both in that moment.

Something had shifted between us after that session. Sitting there eating lunch, listening to his excitement about his work being published, filled me up with such joy and gratitude that my eyes brimmed with tears. "Mom, are you going to cry again?" Josh said, teasing me.

"These are tears of joy," I told him. Though they were also tears of relief, exhaustion and fear. I did not want these few moments of peace to come to an end.

The sun was shining bright in the cloudless sky, illuminating the waiting room at the eye doctor's office. I realized that with the dilation required to check Josh's eyes, the ride back to his facility might be challenging. "I don't have your sunglasses in my car, Josh," I mentioned as I verbalized the tail end of my thoughts.

"Why not?" His tone had changed and his body language had changed, too. He was slumped down in the chair, hunching over his phone.

"Where is that happy-go-lucky kid I just had lunch with?" I thought. He looked over at me, waiting for my response; his eyes looked cold and agitated. "Josh, I haven't had your sunglasses in my car for months."

"Great," he scowled, "just great."

I was thinking the same thing.

The nurse called Josh's name before the conversation could deteriorate any further, and I silently breathed a sigh of relief. Josh seemed to relax as the nurse updated his information. "Any changes in your vision?"

"Nope," Josh responded, "but I'd like to get some colored contacts"

"Really?" I was surprised to hear this.

"Yeah, I thought it would be a good time to make a change. I've never really cared for my brown eyes." The nurse said she'd made a note of it in his chart, but he'd have to speak with the doctor on that matter. Josh's eyes were dilated, and we were moved to another room to wait for the doctor.

"Josh, have you recently had an eye infection?"

The question surprised us both. "Yeah, a few months ago I had pink eye that wouldn't go away," he replied.

It was the doctor's turn to be surprised. "Why didn't you come in to see me then?"

It was too much to try to explain in a few words what had been happening in Josh's life for the past 12 months, so I responded, "Josh was out of town when it happened." It was partially true: the first eye infection occurred while he was in Pennsylvania, but it came back again shortly after he had transferred to his current facility.

"There is scar tissue around his cornea," the doctor continued. "It must have been some infection."

I thought back to the multiple conversations that I had with the on-staff doctors at both residential facilities. They had said that the eye was infected, but there had been no mention of it being serious. I immediately felt guilty, like I had somehow allowed this to happen. What had I missed? How could this be so bad? It was certain that I would be having a conversation with the medical staff that afternoon after I dropped off Josh.

"Can I still get colored contacts?" Josh inquired.

"I'm afraid not, Josh."

"Why not?" I could see Josh was working really hard to keep himself under control.

"The colored contacts don't allow for the eye to breathe well, and with your scar tissue, it would be unhealthy for you to wear them for long periods of time."

Josh was furious, and I was afraid he was going to lash out on the doctor. "What if he wore them occasionally?" I offered, trying to mitigate an explosion.

The whole scenario must have seemed trivial to our doctor, but this was just the type of situation that could set Josh into a full-on rage. When the doctor excused himself to go get another prescription pad, I told Josh I'd call tomorrow and see if I could talk the doctor into a trial if he promised to wear them only an hour or two at a time. Wanting to interrupt the blowout that was most certainly coming, I hoped it was a compromise that would work. It was critical at that point that we finished up and headed back to Josh's facility before something major happened. Josh didn't bring it up again when the doctor returned with his regular prescription.

Josh waited outside while I checked out. Through the window, I could see him pacing. Back and forth, back and forth. He was chewing on his cuticles, a nervous habit he'd had for years. As the receptionist handed me back my credit card and receipt, I took a deep breath and worried about what I was about to face.

"I'm not going back to that place!" Josh was screaming as we got into the car. "Don't take me back there, this is all your fault!"

Locking the doors, I started the car and began driving out of the parking lot. Josh continued screaming. "I am not going back there! I'll jump out of this car right now! I am not kidding!"

Josh unlocked the doors but I relocked them. Panic filled my body. We were approaching an intersection and I realized that if the light remained red, it could mean trouble. I said a silent prayer: "Please turn the light green"

The light changed to green just as we approached the intersection and, without slowing down, I made a right-hand turn and headed towards the highway. Josh was screaming in my face, so close that I could feel his spit sticking to my cheek. "Please let us get to the highway without having to stop," I prayed again. Reasoning with Josh was not working;

he was passed the point of no return with his rage. I didn't know what else to do, so I kept driving while I tried to calm the situation.

Getting us both safely back to the facility was my primary goal. Josh continued to make it clear that he did not want to go back and that he wanted me to take him to his dad's house. There was nothing about this situation that made me feel that he was safe to be anywhere but under the supervision of his residential counselors and medical staff.

The speedometer read 80 mph; everything was a blur as we passed other cars on the highway. "If we get pulled over, at least I will have some help calming Josh down," I thought as I sped towards the facility.

"You can't keep me there! I won't stay! I will run away again!" Josh's threats were getting more desperate. We were almost there. I was holding my breath and praying that we got there safely.

Surprisingly, Josh got right out of the car when we pulled up in front of his cottage. He marched up to the door and rang the buzzer. I followed behind, wary of what would follow, but as the door was opened to him, he walked in and headed right up to his room. I quickly informed the on-staff counselor, Chris, about what had happened and told him I'd be heading over to the administration building to get Josh's medical records and alert his treatment team.

The physician's assistant was in his office and immediately pulled out Josh's records. "Yes, he did have an eye infection when he arrived from Pennsylvania, and we took him to our eye doctor the next day."

I inquired as to whether there was any indication of the serious nature of the infection, but there was not. In the middle of this conversation Kristin, Josh's therapist, joined us in the office. She'd received a call from Josh's cottage and wanted to get more information. As the P.A. made copies of Josh's files, I gave a brief recap of the situation.

Another resident was waiting to speak with the P.A., so I followed Kristin to her office to continue our conversation. "I'm really concerned about him and his safety," I said. Still rattled from the experience, my hands were shaking in my lap as I spoke.

The phone rang, and Kristin shared that it was from Josh's cottage. "Hello? Yes, the mom is still here. Oh really? Okay, I'll let her know" Kristin's face showed more concern than I was expecting. She let out a loud exhale, "Josh's stepmother just came and picked him up."

$$* \; * \; *$$

The following day, Kristin called to inform me that Josh would not be returning. His father had made the decision to withdraw him from care. Since Josh had not harmed himself or threatened suicide over the past 90 days, they were not able to dispute his early discharge, she explained, even though his psychiatrist had been pushing for a June release.

So that was it. The decision was unilateral, and this news left me numb. I was still trying to pick up the pieces from so many other terrifying and heart-wrenching experiences that had occurred over the past 16 months, and suddenly overnight I found myself hurled back into fear and uncertainty once again.

Chapter 29

• • • •

April 2012

It has been just a few weeks since Josh left the residential facility. His treatment team did not feel he was ready; he left nonetheless. I wasn't part of the decision because I would have favored having him stay until the entire treatment team felt he was ready. After everything he'd been through and the stress, worry, and battles to keep him safe, it wasn't a decision I was willing to take lightly.

I haven't slept or even breathed much, for that matter, since that day he was pulled from the program. So much has happened over these past sixteen months. There is so much uncertainty and pain in my heart. Too often, I've felt as though there was a shift coming or a light at the end of the tunnel, only to be thrust back into the deep, dark cycle of this mental health journey.

My current worry and fear doesn't have to do with how much I trust him. I know that he felt ready to transition out of residential treatment. I understand his desire to be home and get on with his life. At this point, he had been hospitalized for more than seven months. Anyone in that position would want to be back home.

I think that things got increasingly more difficult for him when he moved back here. So close to home, and yet it was still out of his reach. The visitations home on the weekends ultimately made it harder and harder *for him to go back into the facility on Monday mornings. I understand all of this and yet, I am scared. It's just too difficult right now to trust that things will be all right. We've all been through so much, Josh included. I'm just not sure right now how I will move forward and heal. I just can't trust that this is the turning point I've dreamt about for months.*

Time will tell, of course. In the meantime, I'm learning to acclimate to this new way of being yet again, and it is taking its toll on me. I want nothing more than for Josh to be safe and healthy and for him to know how much he is loved. Yet, I am unsure what words to use at this point to communicate this wish to him. He is barely talking to me as it is. The only thing that I can do is practice breathing and taking one step at a time. Holding my breath and climbing into my blanket cave will not change the direction of this leg of our journey. Yet I cannot help but feeling, here we go again.

✻ ✻ ✻

That ended up being the last hospitalization and residential stay for Josh. It would take weeks for me to finally trust enough to breathe a bit more freely again. Honestly, it would be months, perhaps years, before I felt that I could fully trust that he was going to be okay. It was in this space of beginning to trust and allow my son to continue his journey to healing that my own healing began.

I thought back to that night so long ago, when I had called out to the Universe for support. I knew that it was time to begin my own deep healing; healing that I had started so long ago and now needed to continue to find my way back to me.

Reflecting back on that night as I called out for help, I remember feeling that something had shifted. In order to find a way to move forward after Josh's ordeal, I knew that I needed to step back and look at my life through the big-picture lens. I took inventory of the amazing blessings that had come into my life since that night I surrendered my path to something bigger than me. I had received so many blessings, even in the dark, heart-wrenching times during those years since.

As I began to trust more in the process of my son's journey and felt safer to begin to explore more of my own healing, I took some time to remember and reflect on how far I'd come; this made me feel somewhat safer and more at ease to tackle this next big step in my journey. Here I was, about as far from paradise as I could have possibly imagined, and I didn't even have a map that could help me find my way back. But I had faith, though not necessarily in the religious sense, but definitely in the spiritual sense.

I had been in what felt to me like the pit of hell before, on a number of occasions. With the right people showing up for me at the right time, I had not only survived, but had learned to thrive as a result. I had every intention of doing it again.

Chapter 30

• • • •

L ife did not, as I had hoped, resume with some semblance of the old normal after Josh left treatment. I was scared of a continuation of the rollercoaster ride that felt unpredictable and unending. More concerning was that Josh was approaching his eighteenth birthday and because he had left treatment against the wishes of his attending team, it would be a very difficult road to get him back into the programs and services if he needed additional support. I had been warned that should he need additional care, many of the adolescent programs that he'd participated in in the past would look at his age and refer him to adult facilities. There would be no continuation of care, and we'd be starting at the beginning once again. The thought of this was overwhelming and exhausting.

When Josh left treatment, it felt like going from 100 mph to a complete stop overnight. While I had learned to take better care of myself during this long crisis, I was still depleted in all aspects of body, mind, and spirit. This shock alone wreaked havoc on my nervous system, and I was burned out. Recognizing this aspect of my own crisis was one thing, but it would still take some time to get back to whole-body wellness. I wasn't sure when I would have the strength to begin that climb.

In the silence of the days that followed, after the abrupt end to the treatment team meetings, counseling sessions, and miscellaneous appointments, there was time to really look at my life, a life that lay partially in shambles around me. I knew that I had to address a number of realities at that point and figure out what pieces should be put back together and what should be left along the road where they had fallen.

The hardest part of that post-treatment time was that I had to face the reality of Josh not coming home to live with me again. Even though the decision had been made more than a year before, he had been hospitalized for most of that time, so the days that followed his discharge offered the first true glimpse of this reality for me.

Weeks passed and I had little to no information about Josh's health or progress. Since the insurance company was billing me for his sessions, I learned that he had been going to therapy. I was glad he was seeing a therapist, especially since his past private-practice therapist opted not to treat him after the way he had chosen to leave residential care. I had also been in contact with Josh's school and his teachers, which provided me with some insight into whether or not he'd be able to complete the school year and move onto his senior year.

The school district thankfully accepted all of the credits that Josh had completed while he was living in the residential facilities, allowing him to enter into the mainstream school as though he'd been there all year. Seeing the way the school adapted and made it possible for Josh to continue his education was a reminder that there had been a few bright spots along the journey. Even with the school's willingness to work with Josh, he had to put effort in, as well. This proved to be quite a challenge. Maybe it was the fact that he'd not been in a standard school environment for the better part of the year or that he truly just didn't see school as a priority, but as the end of the final semester drew near, his chances of passing declined significantly.

On the last day of school, the guidance counselor called as a courtesy. It was too close to call whether or not Josh had done enough to qualify for advancement, and she felt that it was important that we knew upfront. Fear and panic once again overtook my emotions. While Josh didn't think it mattered whether he passed or failed, I was afraid that failure might put him right back into crisis.

Each day when the mail truck pulled up to our house, I'd anxiously sort through the letters looking for his final grading report. The wait was almost too much to bear. "What will I do if he doesn't pass?" I wondered constantly. He'd made it clear that he wasn't going to repeat the grade. I knew in my heart that there wasn't anything I could do to fix this situation, just like there wasn't anything I could have done to fix any of the situations Josh experienced.

Six days after the semester ended, I stood in front of my house with the unopened letter from Josh's school in my hand. For a brief moment, I considered not opening the communication. Realizing that choosing to ignore the reality, whatever it might be, wasn't going to change the outcome. I decided to open the letter. My eyes were darting over the page, trying to quickly find the final grade. There it was: 65.0. Josh had passed by a single point. I exhaled a loud, long sigh that startled a pair of mourning doves in my front dogwood. "Whohoo!" I hollered and called Josh to tell him the news.

$$* \quad * \quad *$$

As summer vacation started, the days felt strangely empty. For the past several years, our summer schedule revolved around Josh's camp employment. He would not be returning to the camp. He said that he didn't want to go back but, after the way things ended the past summer, I imagined that the feeling was mutual. It still left a big whole in my summer plans. The house felt even emptier, and I deeply missed his presence. I was still mourning not just his physical absence but also his choice to detach further from our once close relationship. I held onto hope that one day, he would change his mind and come home.

In the middle of July, on the afternoon I'd said goodbye to a beautiful friend who had succumb to cancer, my doorbell rang. I almost didn't answer - I was exhausted from the heat and had just returned home from her memorial service. The doorbell rang a second time and I forced myself to get out of the chair and answer. Standing on my front step was a man with soft eyes. I didn't know him, but I knew instantly why he was there. "I'm very sorry to do this ma'am." I could tell he was being honest. I reached out and took the paperwork from him. I was being served.

The Request for Child Support Services included a signed affidavit stating that Josh had no intention of ever returning to my home. And that was that.

* * *

My life lay in bits and pieces around me. I was still trying to figure out how to move forward and sort through the hurt, shame, and blame that had accumulated during Josh's crisis. Before I had time to even begin to process, I found myself dealing with yet another situation that created angst and drama in my life.

As a result of the custody case involving my older son some years earlier, I was solely and financially responsible for Josh and all of his needs. Because of this, the new support case would take more than eighteen months to settle. The entire process served to drive a bigger wedge between my children and me.

Over those eighteen months, I had a chance to put some of the pieces of my life back together. I was able to begin to heal some of the relationships that had fallen away, choose to lovingly close the door on others and physically heal my worn-out body. The heartbreak over my son leaving my home and the subsequent estrangement by both my children would not, however, be something that could immediately be healed. In fact, as I write this, I still have very little relationship with both my children today. I have mourned and mourned this truth.

For many months, I kept the estrangement from my children a secret. Even as I had faced, head-on, the stigma, blame, and shame in relation to Josh's mental illness, the thought of sharing with anyone that I was a mother who did not have a relationship with her children was almost too much to bear. Even more though, the absolute heartbreak, the way my heart shattered again in ways that I could not have imagined, was just too hard to speak about. I finally got to a point, though, where I needed to tell the truth about my situation not because anyone needed to know particularly, but because I needed to speak it out loud.

This wasn't the first time I felt strongly about sharing my experiences out loud. As Josh's situation stabilized, I realized that I had two choices: I could pick up the pieces and go on with my life as though nothing had happened or I could use the experience to help others. Since it had been so difficult for me to find support and guidance during Josh's crisis, the choice was easy. I started a blog and began to share my story, lessons learned and pitfalls of supporting a loved one through crisis.

Since I had been sharing more and more of my vulnerable, raw and real story with my blog readers, I decided to come out to them first - as a Childless Mother.

* * *

April 2014

I have been holding something in for a long time, I wonder if anyone else would be able to relate to this. Lately, it's been weighing heavily on my mind. Every time someone inquires about my family and how things are going, I feel like I am not able to be 100% truthful. I've decided that it is time to come clean with you all, so that you know what my truth is; truth is freeing.

If you have been reading my blog for a while or even if you are a new reader, you'll know that I openly discuss and face mental health issues and the stigma associated with mental health crises head on. This situation is even more personal and in many ways as stigma-laden as the subject that I have been writing about for several years now, which is why I have kept it quiet until now

Ok, here I go....

*I am a **childless mother.***

For the past six months, and honestly on and off over the past several years, my children have made the choice to sever their relationships with me.

My older son, whom I have shared little about on the blog, has completely shut me out of his life. During this time, he graduated from college, started at a new school to pursue his bachelor's degree and let Christmas come and go without a word. My younger son will respond to a text now and again and did stop by for a visit on Christmas morning, but he also made it very clear that he does not feel he can have a relationship with me right now.

Whoa! Right? What kind of mother loses her relationship with not one but both of her children? This kind of mother, the kind who loves unconditionally, who refuses to enable unhealthy behavior, who chooses to be a parent over being a friend, and who believes in accountability and facing consequences. These are among the very reasons why my children are choosing not to have a relationship with me right now.

I cannot begin to put into words the depth of pain and grief that I have been feeling and working through over these past several months. There are days where I truly feel like I am mourning a death and at times find myself on my knees at the edge of the pit of hell and not sure how to find my way back.

But, I am healing. It will take me some time to piece my heart back together and, while it's not completely healed, the healing has begun.

Chapter 31

• • • •

After a serious life event, many people choose to take a fresh look at their lives. I found this to be true for me, as well. As I emerged from the foggy brain state where I had existed during much of Josh's crisis, focusing on only those things that were absolutely critical, I realized that I had been so changed by the process that nothing in my life was the same. To move forward, I had to look long and hard at my beliefs and the stories that I had been carrying with me for much of my life. I looked at the people in my life, deciding who was positively in my space and who, for whatever reason, no longer resonated with who I had become or what I wanted for my future.

I had to face up to the fact that my career was no longer satisfying. It had once felt like it was my life purpose and, for a long time, I thought I was truly on my path. I believed for many years that I was going to continue to climb the corporate ladder, rising to higher and higher rungs because I was a hard worker and I was good at my job. I really couldn't picture myself doing anything else. I liked leading people. I liked working with teams. Yet even before Josh's crisis, I recognized that things had started changing; the work that had once brought me great pride and enjoyment had become tedious, unfulfilling and, at times, made me seriously wonder what the hell I was thinking.

I believe that this line of self-questioning came up because my soul was knocking on my door, asking me why I wasn't doing something I enjoyed passionately. My career had lost its luster, but I was still in a bit of denial. Before Josh's crisis, I became a certified life and corporate coach and started practicing part-time. I found that I was passionate about this work, but I could not easily see how I could turn it into a full-time career. It didn't fit into my vision of how I expected my career path to unfold. I wasn't ready to make a change or take a risk.

I was full of excuses, and those excuses kept me stuck. Even the crisis was an excuse to stay put on my current career path, though the thought of dealing with a career move in the midst of balancing the enormous responsibilities associated with supporting Josh would likely not have been a positive experience.

While my soul may have been knocking, I hadn't been ready to answer to the door. Instead I pushed on, plowed through and rationalized all the reasons why I needed to give my job another chance. "I haven't tried hard enough," I thought. "Now that Josh isn't in crisis, I can really give this my all and make this work."

I stuck with the job and worked harder to prove my worth because I told myself that this is what you do. What I didn't realize was that I was stuck in the story that life was hard, grueling, and it beat you down. There was no consideration given to the fact that perhaps my thought process was flawed. Given all that I had been through over the past few years, it is no wonder that I held fast and true to this belief.

I believed that purpose was something you either had or you didn't. There I was, coming out the other side of the hardest, most heartbreaking years of my life while going through the career motions, and I figured if I didn't consider that role to be my true purpose any longer, maybe I really didn't have one. Finding my purpose stopped being a factor in my decision to continue in my current role. So I soldiered on.

Fast-forward one year later, and I found myself physically ill and emotionally wrung out. I knew that I could no longer pretend that everything was fine. I began to look at other employment options and possibilities, but nothing I found felt right. Then, suddenly, overnight, everything changed.

Chapter 32

• • • •

"You better lose yourself in the music, the moment

You own it, you better never let it go

You only get one shot, do not miss your chance to blow

This opportunity comes once in a lifetime"

- Eminem

S o here I am quoting Eminem, right? This song and its exclamation, "Success is my only motherf'ing option" got me through some really tough days when Josh was in the hospital. I would scream the lyrics at the top of my lungs as I drove back and forth for visitation or when I was driving to one of the hundreds of treatment team or counseling sessions that I participated in with him.

The company that I was working for was being sold and I was in essence sold along with it. The turmoil and undermining that had been occurring over the previous couple of years, which I had all but chosen to ignore because I was dealing with my own sets of personal crises, was coming to a head.

At first, I looked at this as an opportunity to re-prove myself and get back into the game in a stronger leadership capacity. I saw the initial change as positive and felt like, with my background and experience, I could turn this into a great new chapter and a rebirth of my career. Early on, it felt like the perfect progression from the old to the new, a great delineation point and a fresh start. I saw this as my chance to once again own it and not let the opportunity slip away.

Success was my only motherf'ing option; failure was not.

Chapter 33

• • • •

As I started down the path of my new position with this new company, I realized that there was so much about how things had played out before, during, and after the transition that left a bad taste in my mouth. What started out looking like a positive experience turned into chaos, and I felt like I was right back on the road to the pit of hell even as I tried, pushed, and forced myself eighteen to twenty hours a day to do the impossible. I knew, even at the beginning, that my work was not appreciated but, even more, I began to see how truly out of synch my career was with what my soul wanted to do.

My son's crisis certainly taught me many things, but one important lesson was that life's too short to be spending time doing what does not make your soul happy. I knew it before my son's crisis too, but I often have a way of ignoring or justifying why I choose to not honor my soul's desires. When I realized that this was absolutely not the job nor the company for me, I also realized I felt even more stuck than I had the year prior. Then I had obligations, I couldn't make rash decisions; I felt like there was no exit strategy available to me.

Now, I had a few things going for me, though. The first was that Josh was no longer deep in his crisis and as a result of the child support case, his father covered his health insurance. Maintaining my insurance had been a big concern throughout the months Josh was hospitalized and in treatment. Secondly, I knew that any position that I could find would be a breath of fresh air compared to staying put in that unfulfilling and exhausting job. So while the scarcity fear factor spread around my company like wild fire with whispers of, "There are no jobs out there," or "It is a very bad time to be unemployed," I knew without a doubt that even if I had to change my lifestyle, it would be worth it to move out of that toxic environment.

With the number of hours I was working, there was little left for anything else in my life, and job searching was an exhausting proposition. So, for many months, I ignored the fact that I knew I needed to make a change. Even as I went through this situation and could see how the similarities between where I was at that moment and where I had been with my son in his crisis, I still chose not to address it for several months.

The Universe, as I have learned, has a way of getting my attention, though, and the longer I dug in my heels, thinking that I was going to "show them" that I was the right person for the job, the more the Universe created situations in my life in hopes of getting my attention.

It was no surprise when I developed a serious lung infection. My poor diet, lack of exercise and thousands of airline miles per week caught up with me with a vengeance. The big turning point for me came when I was sitting in the office at 7:00 pm, figuring I could still work another hour before the Urgent Care clinic would be closing. It suddenly hit me that I was one of the last people in the office, and I was really sick.

Within minutes of checking into the Urgent Care that night, I had been given two steroid breathing treatments and instructions to check myself into the hospital the next morning if my lungs had not opened up.

Here I was, ignoring all of the self-care lessons that were so hard-learned during Josh's crisis. I had fought to get myself healthy and keep myself healthy for my son, but when it came to fighting to keep myself healthy for me, I fell down on the job completely. Waking up in the middle of my own health crisis was more than an eye opener for me.

It spoke volumes about how I was willing put my needs and my health aside to prove once again my own personal worth.

I started with very practical actions; I began applying for positions with companies for a similar position. Even as I did this, I recognized that I disliked the work I was doing, but I had convinced myself that if I could at least get a similar job with a new company, it might give me some breathing room to explore what my next steps were in the grander scheme of my life purpose.

I truly loved the coaching, writing and advocating work that I was doing part-time, but never considered it a possibility. The concept that I could do work that bridged my passion and my creativity while allowing me to meet my financial obligations wasn't even on my radar at that point.

I could go into a long, drawn-out story about how I applied to numerous companies all across the country, but it was pretty mundane. Suffice it to say, I applied for many open positions, heard back from a few and ended up with one very promising interview.

The day I was told to expect the offer, I instead got a phone call letting me know that the CEO of the company had put all hiring on hold. I knew at that moment that I had to make a bold decision to honor myself and begin to thrive once again in my life, especially since I had been barely surviving for months.

Often in the coaching work that I do, my clients ask how can they be certain that taking a big bold leap will turn out okay. The honest answer is that there are no guarantees. Taking a leap of faith and jumping without a net doesn't mean that life will be easy or that there won't be lessons to learn and bumps in the road; on the contrary, bumps and bruises are to be expected. It is not the safest route. Often, taking risks and blazing a new trail is about as scary as one could imagine.

Recognizing that I had already survived and thrived due to some pretty scary experiences in my life made my decision easier. More than that, I knew that if I didn't make a radical change, life would most likely serve me up a radical change anyway. I decided that it was best to cave in early and listen to my soul's guidance before I was forced to look at what wasn't working in my life.

Chapter 34

• • • •

April 2014

A week ago, after months of contemplation and discussion, I've made the decision to walk away from my job. Even writing this feels surreal. I am not just walking away from a job, but I'm walking away from my livelihood. I am not independently wealthy, nor do I have an inheritance that will keep me safe and secure for the rest of my days. I am like most, living the "American Dream." I'm obligated up to my eyeballs with a mortgage, child support, credit card debt and the like. And yet here I am, just hours away from giving my company two weeks' notice, knowing that there is a chance I will be out of a job within minutes of making my decision known.

To say that I am not a little freaked out would be a lie. There are parts of me that know for certain that I am making the right decision. But my mind and its pesky sidekick fear are trying their damnedest to get me riled up. While I've been trying to ignore it over the past few days, I cannot disregard how it is showing up physically in my body. Yesterday and today, my lungs have been really tight, and I have been having extreme headaches and body aches, as well. I have a sense that once I communicate my intentions to my leadership, I will feel much better.

I want so much to feel good about my decision and "know" that things will be full of grace and ease going forward. It feels as though I'm pulling off the Band-Aid on one very hairy arm. I'm choosing to do it on my time and in my way though, and not waiting for it to be pulled off by someone else. I am taking control of my life and announcing quite loudly and boldly, "This path no longer serves me," and then I am choosing a path that does serve me. I am choosing a nurturing path, a path of soul-filling work and life-affirming adventures. I am ready. Today and the day after this and the day after that... I am ready. The only thing left to do is turn in my resignation.

I decided that I want to communicate my resignation over the phone to my leadership. A few friends asked me why I didn't just send a memo and be done with it, but I just don't feel like that is the best way for me to do this. It doesn't matter what others would do, it only matters that I feel I'm doing it in the best way for me.

As I reflect back on this experience, I realize how grateful I am for the way this entire process has played out. I am learning a lot about myself and about allowing things to unfold in ways that I may not be expecting. It has been a big lesson in patience and trust.

For now the waiting is over and it's time to take the leap. And away I go!

Chapter 35

• • • •

had always heard that if the choices a person makes are truly in alignment with their highest path, that doors would open almost effortlessly for them. As I found myself newly "retired," I never once wondered if leaving my career was the wrong decision. From the very first day, I knew it was right. I just felt it in my soul.

Those first weeks after my resignation were dedicated to recuperation. It had been years since I had the space to rest, and I'm not sure if ever there was a time that I purposefully looked at my life to see what else I might want to do for a living. I had the coaching and advocacy work that I had been doing throughout the past several years, so I knew that was my starting point. I loved the work and I felt that it was so connected to what I was meant to be doing.

As I looked back over the numerous crises that I had faced in the years prior to leaving my job, one thing became very clear to me: those experiences, the lessons that I learned and the pitfalls I had stumbled upon were not for me to keep to myself. I truly needed to know that I had gone through those dark times, endured the heartbreak and the disappointment, the fear and the hopelessness, so that I could help support others who had walked or would walk a similar path.

I decided that the only next steps that made sense to me was to surrender to the unknown and start saying "yes" to all opportunities that came my way. I was excited and nervous to see what would unfold, but I knew that I truly needed to take the time to explore whatever adventures were out there.

All that time on my hands also gave me the space - sometimes unwanted - to feel the impact of the past few years. Having basically jumped from my son's exit from treatment to the child support court case and then into the extensive and exhausting corporate role, I hadn't really had a chance to feel or mourn some of the big changes that had occurred. First and foremost was the loss of the relationship with not one but both of my children. I knew that it needed to play out the way it did, yet when I finally allowed myself to feel the whole of it, it nearly destroyed me. That is the thing with being so busy- it kept me from having the time to feel or process the big emotional things in my life. This is not to say that I wasn't mourning the losses, but it was sporadic. This time meant truly feeling it all. And thank goodness, it also meant healing so much of it.

As I began my journey into the unknown, I realized that I had two options: I could look at everything as opportunity and possibility, or I could look at nothing that way. I knew that I wanted a better way to live my life and a more soul-connected avenue for sharing my talents with the world. I didn't have to wait long for the Universe to provide me with opportunities to say, "Yes."

In fact, I was blessed with a number of wonderful opportunities right away. The first was a weekend yoga festival with a group of women whom I did not know well but who helped me to create a heart-opening and soul-healing experience. Even though I cried through many of the yoga classes that I participated in during that weekend, the whole experience felt perfectly timed. I was blessed to have spent it with a beautiful group of soulful women, which made the entire weekend that much more rich and lovely. Around that same time, a friend asked me to consider traveling to California to attend a blogging conference. I had considered attending earlier in the year, and had all but decided that I was going to pass on it. Something inside me felt that, given my current situation, it was a perfect time to go. So I reconsidered the opportunity and said, "Yes."

In the days leading up to my trip to the blogging conference, I was approached to participate in a book anthology project. I had heard about the project earlier in the year from a close friend of mine but, at that time, I was so deep in my own muck, the thought of participating in one more project seemed daunting and overwhelming. The beauty of this life is that often, if an opportunity is truly meant for us, it will circle around again. As luck would have it, when I was approached a second time about the possibility of joining in, I was ready and willing to say, "Yes." It was a bold "yes" even for me, since the final draft of my submission was due just five days after I agreed to join the project. To add to the challenge, I was leaving for California three days later. However, I truly believe that I was following my intuition and listening to my soul when I said, "Yes," and, as I did, things began to unfold. The entire book submission came together on my flight from New York to California. I put the finishing touches on my draft when I got to the hotel and finalized my submission two days prior to the deadline.

I was in the flow; I was following my breadcrumbs one at a time. I didn't know where I was going or how it would all play out, but I knew that if I was truly serious about taking my message and my gifts out into the world, I needed to rely on a higher knowing and not just my brain alone.

It is in these moments of realization where I can see how my son's crisis and the journey it took me on helped me to learn so much about trust. I didn't know the ending to my son's story while I was in the middle of it, and even now his journey is far from over, but I knew that I had to take one step at a time and trust that I would know what to do next. Here I was again, walking a similar path; however, this time it felt much gentler than when I had experienced it before.

The trip to the blogger conference ended up being a major turning point. First, I was able to get very clear on what direction I wanted to take both my blog and my business. During this time, I mapped out my vision for what my new branding would be, what my primary service offerings would encompass and how I would wrap up all of this development in an extremely short timeframe so that I could align the launch of my business with the release of the anthology. I had just under 6 weeks to pull it all together in order to meet this compressed timeline.

Another lesson that I learned through my son's crisis was tenacity and how to trust my ability to get things done when time was of the essence. I arrived home from the conference ready to get started. Just to add to the adventure, I also came home from this trip with a newly inspired idea to move to the west coast.

My love affair with California, and most specifically the Bay Area, had started years ago, just after high school when a close friend made the bold move out west. Over the last decade or so, Pete and I traveled out there at least once yearly for vacation and, with each trip, my love for the area grew deeper. We always spoke about someday making the move, but the timing had not been right to do it until now.

So in the midst of launching my business, my website, and a book, we made the decision to speak to a realtor about putting our home on the market. Even though I was saying, "Yes," to the move, I still wanted to take it one step at a time. The house went on the market a couple weeks later, went under contract in four days, and away we went - saying "Yes" all along the path.

I want to stop here for a moment, because I have a tendency to get a bit carried away when I tell this story. If I were to explain what was happening and how it all felt during this timeframe, the only way that I can really describe it is to say that it felt like I had a fire hose at my back, pushing me forward at speeds that often took my breath away. It was almost unbelievable the way that everything lined up and how the doors blew open every time that I said, "Yes," to what felt absolutely right for my next steps.

As wonderful and magical as this experience was, there were elements of it that were truly heartbreaking for me. I was leaving my home, the only city that I had ever lived in. My family resided in this place and my roots ran deep and wide in that city. The toughest part of the decision was that it was my children's home, as well. There was a security for me in knowing that they were only a few towns away if anything major happened or if, one day, they decided to have a relationship with me again. This was a big decision. I had to come face to face with the reality that by staying, living on a prayer that my children might decide to reunite with me, I would not be honoring myself. I wasn't moving because they chose this path. Josh had been stable for a couple of years and, given the circumstances, I decided that it was time to choose what was next for me based on having the space and the freedom to choose to stay or go.

Chapter 36

• • • •

October 2014

I wonder if it is possible to put into words the whirlwind Grand Adventure I have been on since that early August day when I said to Pete, "Why don't we put the house on the market and see what happens?"

It has felt like a bright light, a whooosh and a snap. Of course, the adventure has been much more than that. In fact, it has been a complete lane change.

Less than six weeks after our house went on the market, I found myself pulling out of my driveway for the last time, prepping for a 2800-mile trek across the country. The emotions that I've experienced during this time have felt like quite a rollercoaster ride. Going from excited to petrified, happy to distraught, back and forth and up and down. Exhausting.

I observed a number of things about myself during this process. For one, I realize that I was more attached to some of my material possessions than I could have ever imagined. I had heart palpitations when I realized that we were going to be selling our gas grill or that I was going to have to let go of certain pieces of furniture that we were not going to have room for in our new, much smaller home.

There were bigger things I had to let go of, too. Having to make decisions around which of my children's toys, art projects, and school papers would make the move and which would not caused me to shed lots of tears. Then there was the house, my beautiful home. It was my dream home from the moment I stepped foot in it and still held that place in my soul when I closed the garage door for the last time. I have to keep reminding myself that these are things, just things, and it was time to let them all go. I need to keep remembering that the memories and connection to these things will still live on in my heart.

What has been even more challenging and emotional for me were the many good-byes and "see you later's" that I had to say to my children, family and friends, many of whom helped keep me grounded during some of the most difficult years of my life.

I know it's best to focus on the positive. This is a completely fresh slate, a new start. I am still finding my bearings and, at times, I feel overwhelmed by the whole adventure. I am a bit homesick as well, but am hopeful and excited to keep moving forward with my work, advocacy support, and writing projects. The bonus is in knowing that I won't be shoveling out from under 100-plus inches of snow this coming winter; that is good for my soul and spirit!

I've learned a lot in this twelve-week period, and I think in some ways even now I'm still sorting it out and feeling all of it. One thing that I can say for certain is that sometimes you have to leave it behind before you can move it forward. Time will tell and life will unfold, one-step or giant leap at a time.

✳ ✳ ✳

The fascinating part of this story is that many things were happening during this time concurrently. All were things that I had said "Yes" to, but I hadn't thought they'd all occur in the same window of time. In the midst of the move, my website and book launched, and my coaching calendar began to fill up almost immediately.

Just a short six months after my decision to walk away from a career that no longer served me, I was living the life of my dreams. I can see how pivotal my choices had been after Josh's crisis, especially choosing to heal the deep pain and inaccurate beliefs that were keeping me stuck in a life that no longer served me. Through it, I learned the most important lesson of all: I learned to truly love myself.

As I sit back and remember the way that the pieces came together, I almost find it hard to believe. Yet, all I need to do is look up and see San Francisco out my window to remember that it all really happened. I've come just a bit closer to paradise. What a wild ride indeed.

The End

Epilogue

• • • •

As I started down the long road of my son's health crisis, I couldn't believe the number of times I tripped and fell into something where I had no idea I needed to watch out for danger. I was, as many would be, fully immersed in the experience, focusing on what my son needed to keep him safe and alive. I thought that the medical community was the expert, that I was somehow to blame for the situation; I felt that everything should come secondary, including my health and well being, in order to ensure that my son was supported. And that's not all: I found myself giving my power away over and over again, even when I knew that there was a better way to support my son; ways that worked with him and his specific needs.

Then one day I stopped. I remembered that I knew my son better than any of his treatment team members and I knew myself better than the victim game I was playing. I took a huge step back and realized that in order to support my son and myself through the crisis, things were going to need to change.

This change was a process; I didn't realize it all at once. Slowly over time, I became more and more aware of cases where I was falling into old, unhealthy patterns while dealing with challenges that were landing on my path. To say I handled everything perfectly would be an overestimation; I mean, really, what is perfect anyway? But what I found was that being aware of these pitfalls and finding ways to manage through them or avoid them all together became my best course of action.

The thing about going through a crisis like this is that along the way I've learned so many important lessons. Often when a crisis is over, there is a desire to get back to a "normal" life and put the crisis as far behind as possible. I cannot help but think that when that occurs, there is so much information and guidance that gets buried right there instead of it being paid forward to give some insight and support to those who are still in the midst of a similar crisis.

While there were many lessons that I learned during the course of this crisis, here are some of the big pitfalls that I encountered and what I did to change course:

Giving away power: Whether you are the parent or primary caregiver for a person in crisis, remember that you know the patient better than any doctor or treatment team can. There are normal assumptions and processes followed by facilities and attending physicians, but they are broad and not applicable to every patient. If a recommendation or course of action doesn't feel "right" to you, speak up and discuss your concerns. Even if your initial concerns are not taken seriously, do not give up your power or concede to treatment or programs that you know don't meet the need. In my situation, I really forced myself to speak up when something didn't feel right to me. Most times my input was welcome, and other times it took a few firm discussions before my input was taken into account. Either way, I realized that I was a partner in my son's treatment, and that meant that my input was valid and necessary to his care.

Turning on yourself: Many caregivers find that there is enough blame and shame to go around, especially in a mental health situation. One surprising realization for me was finding that stigma existed within the medical facility setting. I always assumed that in that environment, the care providers somehow "got it" more than the average person. This worked to only reinforce the belief that I had done something very wrong to cause the situation with my son. I turned on myself. Turning on yourself, punishing yourself through negative thoughts, blaming words, and withdrawing from life will not make your loved one any better. However, over time, it will deplete your health and you may find yourself in need of support, as well. It took me quite a while to stop blaming myself and to start learning to love and accept the way things were playing out.

Ignoring Self Care: During times of crisis, it is critical to take care of yourself mentally, physically, and emotionally. Believe me, I spent several months on the couch with the covers pulled over my head, wanting nothing more than the situation to resolve and life to go back to normal. I stopped making time for sleep, for healthy meals, and for exercise. By chance, I came across an article sharing grim statics regarding caregivers who do not take care of themselves. The bottom line was that in addition to truly not being able to be present for their loved ones, many would likely find themselves faced with a severe illness or disease 18 months post-crisis. Reading these statistics was a huge eye-opener for me and, shortly after, I joined a 40-day yoga program and eventually added running into my weekly routine. I firmly believe these steps helped me be more engaged with my son's treatment and has kept me relatively healthy through the months that followed.

Staying Silent: Not sharing the fact that you are going through a health crisis does not help anyone. Isolation and shame only create more isolation and shame, which can lead to depression and physical health issues. Even if you are uncertain about sharing your story with friends or family members, there are people who can listen in a non-judgmental way. Lean on someone who you know can listen, call a helpline, find a support group or contact an advocate in your area or online. I initially thought that it was best to keep my son's situation to myself, but once the reality of the illness became apparent, I found that the support I could get from family and friends was very helpful. I was also looking, desperately at times, to find others who were going through the same situation as me, hoping that I could talk to someone who truly understood what I was feeling. I didn't find many who were willing to talk, but instead I found that there was much benefit in telling my story to others.

Going into denial: As someone who has experience deep, dark days of caregiving, I can say firsthand that when you're in the middle of it, you want nothing more than to have it resolved. A light at the end of the tunnel is all you hope for and then, one day, everything feels back to "normal" and you breathe deeply. However, denial can creep in slowly. You begin to start looking at things and rationalizing how they are not really red flags. Staying on this road can lead to a situation where the rug is pulled out from under you and you're left rubbing your scraped elbows and trying to figure out what the heck happened. I learned early on in my son's crisis to identify the signs of denial and begin immediately to call it by name. This didn't necessarily change the situations I faced as we rode the rollercoaster of mental health uncertainty, but it allowed me to be eyes-wide-open when the next upside down loop-de-loop came along.

Accepting "No" as the answer: Caregivers in most cases not only deal with the physical needs of their loved ones, but also the logistics of care such as insurance claims, discharge planning, and managing levels of service required for patient care. The systems that "pay out" money for care are set up as profit centers. That means that their goal, just as any corporation's, is to ultimately make money for their top executives and shareholders. Given this, I found that in most cases, "No" will be the first answer when any additional coverage expense is required. Whether the request is for extending inpatient stay, treatment programs, medication changes, and long-term care accommodations, even if when it was recommended by the attending physicians, the answer we got most often was, "No." I found myself on numerous occasions during

Amy White

my son's hospitalizations and residential stays having to go toe-to-toe with the managed-service provider responsible for approving the funds to allow for my son's continued care. It took quite a fight to get the insurance company and managed-care providers to agree to continue to support my son.

Often as caregivers, we have enough ammunition to beat up on and berate ourselves for all of the places we have not done enough to support our loved ones. This information is not about giving you more ways to recognize where you have failed, it is about allowing you to see the possibility and opportunity in taking care of yourself and keeping yourself healthy and engaged during the course of crisis. These pitfalls were the culmination of more than a solid year of tripping, falling, and getting myself back up and into the game. Take one step at a time, that's all you need to do.

Acknowledgements

• • • •

As a result of this experience and the experiences that followed my son's crisis, I continue to learn so much about myself and heal so many deep-rooted wounds. I acknowledge and recognize every single person who played a role on this journey and their contribution to my growth and transformation. While not all interactions were positive, the lessons and learning that took place as a result were profoundly healing.

I want to start by thanking Josh for his willingness to allow parts of his story to be told in such a public format. I acknowledge both my children for their courage to follow their hearts and go after their dreams regardless of the bumpy path. I am incredibly proud of both of you. My love for you will never waiver, no matter what the future holds.

To my husband, Peter, thank you for being a soft place for me to land and for supporting me through this journey and beyond. Thank you for giving me the space to heal and transform and for your willingness to grow along side me. My love for you runs deep and wide, always.

To my parents, Dick and Kathy, for loving me in all the ways that you do. And to Brian, Sara and Amanda, I am equally grateful for each of you. I am forever thankful that I "picked" you to be my family.

To all the doctors, treatment team members and support personnel that were involved in Josh's care before, during and after his crisis, thank you. Without your support Josh may not be with us today. A special shout out to our family advocate, Julie, even though our time together was limited, knowing that I had someone in my court who understood what I was experiencing was appreciated beyond words.

To Joan Nichols and the Inspire Yoga community: practicing with you in that amazing, healing space saved my life and brought me through the crisis healthier that I could have imagined possible. There really is no place like Om.

To my fabulous running community: Laurie, Gail, Suzanne, Molly, Maureen, Richa, Renee, and the rest of the Moms Run This Town crew (on both coasts), you may not have known the healing that was taking place along the many miles we've spent together but your presence, support and willingness to allow me to share my stories has and continues to deeply impact my life.

To my soul sisters near and far, you know who you are! I could never have imagined being surrounded by such an amazing, diverse group of soulful women from all around the globe. Thank you for the support, meals, hugs, check-in Skype calls, prayers, blessings and good juju during and after the crisis. I bow to each of you in gratitude for the gifts, support and love you share with me.

A special thank you to Lauren Sarat, for the masterful editing, wisdom and guidance that helped me frame this story in a way that truly honored the journey. And finally to the team at Motivational Press, thank you for believing in the power of this story, for putting the polish on the final product and bringing it together into this beautiful package.

About the Author

• • • •

Amy White is an International Best-selling author, Caregiver Champion and Intuitive Life Coach who transitioned out of Corporate America to pursue her passion advocating and championing for caregivers after her personal experience supporting her teenage son through a terrifying mental health crisis.

Amy writes the blog *Far From Paradise*; sharing the lessons, challenges, insights and heartache, as well as her own personal healing journey, following her son's breakdown. She hopes that her story about fighting stigma, navigating the mental health services maze and focusing on her own emotional healing will provide a beacon of hope and light for those who are working to support a loved one or themselves on the path to health and wellness.

In 2014, Amy co-authored the International Best Seller, Bold is Beautiful Breakthrough to Business Strategies sharing her story of leaving her career to pursue her dream of coaching and advocating for parents, caregivers and those transitioning through life's challenges and crises.

Amy is also a mental wellness advocate and speaker who works with parents and caregivers helping them to find the best path through the confusing and challenging maze of mental health care.

Amy lives in the San Francisco Bay Area with her husband Peter and dog Quinn and recently her son Josh has come for an extended stay. The journey continues...

www.farfromparadise.org

Facebook: FarFromParadise

Twitter: FarfrmParadise

Twitter: Mzamywhite

Instagram: Mzamywhite

Email: AskAmyWhite@gmail.com

CPSIA information can be obtained
at www.ICGtesting.com
Printed in the USA
FSOW04n0528260716
22974FS